INSIGHTS

TO KITCHEN DESIGN

I0089885

40+ Years in the World of a Design-led Kitchen Specialist

James R.A. Herriot

INSIGHTS

TO KITCHEN DESIGN

40+ Years in the World of a
Design-led Kitchen Specialist

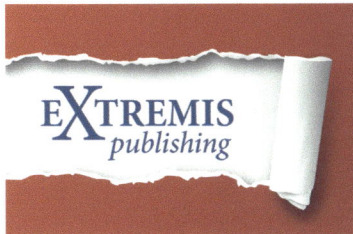

EXTREMIS
publishing

James R.A. Herriot

Insights to Kitchen Design is
dedicated to an amazing Team effort
encompassing a great many years

Embarking on a career in kitchen
design is fascinating & fulfilling...
It will involve time, effort &
perseverance, but will prove
well worthwhile

Insights to Kitchen Design is
dedicated to an amazing Team
effort encompassing a great
many years. Without fellow
Callerton colleagues (past
and present), from within the
organisation and in conjunction
with our National Network of
Design-led Kitchen Specialists,
plus the additional aspect of
partnerships and relationships
with our many Suppliers and
Service Providers – Insights
would not have come to fruition.
Without the many Industry
colleagues I've interacted with
over 40+ years the opportunity
to learn my craft would not have
come about - hence dedicating
the book to them.

Also I'd like to take the
opportunity to dedicate
Insights to all those more
recent recruits to the Design-led
Kitchen Specialist World -
as well as those investigating
the possibility of embarking
on a fascinating and fulfilling
career. It will involve time,
effort and perseverance (and
with the benefit of hindsight)
I can assure those who stay
the course, this will prove
well worthwhile.

DEDICATION

ACKNOWL-EDGEMENTS

I would like to acknowledge the input and efforts of various people without whom Insights to Kitchen Design would not have come to fruition and be published. So a massive thank you to: -

David Knaggs my friend and colleague – originally my apprentice/protégé but now the master. His support and input to this project has been incredible and without his hard work, dedication, skill, ability and input - I can hand on heart tell you, you would not be reading these words.

Julie and Tom Christie the founders of award winning Extremis Publishing have been an essential ingredient and without their belief and support - Insights would not now be in print.

The efforts of various members of Callerton's pre-production Team need to be recognised and acknowledged: Tom, Dominic and Lewis, along with input from my long-time business partner Gordon in relation to producing the 3D CAD drawings for the forty alternative designs.

A massive thank you to David Knaggs, my friend & colleague, originally my apprentice/protégé but now the master

Without the belief & support of Julie & Tom Christie, Insights would not now be in print

Tom, Dominic & Lewis, along with input from my long-time business partner Gordon

ABOUT

THE AUTHOR

To gain an insight as to the author's credentials to write a book in relation to the Design-led Kitchen Specialist World: -

The following words came from Martin Allan-Smith (Editor of Designerati Magazine) when presenting James with the 2023 award for 'Services to the Industry' at their spectacular Designerati Awards event held at the iconic venue of Wembley Stadium (London).

Our Service to the Industry honour is reserved for an individual whose efforts in the sector extends way beyond the norm in terms of the wider impact that their work has had on the industry.

d

awards 2023

WINNER

SERVICES TO
THE INDUSTRY

This year's winner has had an incredible career in kitchens, in which he has stayed true to a set of core visions and beliefs that have stood the test of time.

It is a career that began with property development in the 1970s, but soon transitioned to a focus on kitchens in the early 80s. He and his business partner spotted what they considered to be a few gaps in the industry's offering at the time, so they set about creating their own new kitchen business, prioritising practicality, design, and installation.

The business faced significant hurdles and challenges along the way, such as recession and market uncertainty, but innovation was always their main objective. Our recipient and his business partner won a BBC competition, the 'Make it in Business' awards which gave them some prime time exposure and perhaps some early reassurance that they were very much on the right track.

As I mentioned, that 'test of time' is perhaps the key point to emphasise here. The company that he co-founded celebrated its 40th anniversary this year. And I think everyone here appreciates what a remarkable achievement in itself that is.

It has been done in no small part due to an emphasis on partnership and collaboration, not least with a long-established network of retailers – built up over time through trust and close working relationships – who share this manufacturer's passion for quality and excellence.

Partnership too with other suppliers, helping to co-ordinate a group of key brands to combine resources and ideas on marketing the three core pillars of successful kitchen projects: great design, great products, and great project management.

Our recipient has contributed more widely too, as a former chairman of the KBSA with a genuine and personal passion for education and training within the industry.

Recently stepping down as chairman of the company he co-founded, he has recently turned his considerable skills to writing, penning a book during the pandemic called 'The Sabbatical', a poignant letter to his grandchildren juxtaposing the highs of life with its inevitable lows.

And readers will soon be treated to another tome – Insights to Kitchen Design – encapsulating this man's passion and vast experience in the world of kitchen design, and showcasing the multitude of possibilities that lie within each and every given space. It promises to be a fascinating read for designers and homeowners alike.

Sharing his perspectives in this way is also very much in-keeping with the philosophy that he and business partner Gordon Stanger-Leathes have strived for since founding Callerton 40 years ago – based on the aim of … Turning Dreams to Reality.

An industry visionary and pioneer, please welcome him to the stage to receive the Services to the Industry Award – Mr JAMES HERRIOT.

Martin Allan-Smith
Editor of Designerati Magazine

Insights to Kitchen Design: 40+ Years in the World of a Design-Led Kitchen Specialist by James R.A. Herriot.

First edition published in Great Britain in 2024 by Extremis Publishing Ltd., Suite 218, Castle House, 1 Baker Street, Stirling, FK8 1AL, United Kingdom.
www.extremispublishing.com

Extremis Publishing is a Private Limited Company registered in Scotland (SC509983) whose Registered Office is Suite 218, Castle House, 1 Baker Street, Stirling, FK8 1AL, United Kingdom.

Copyright © James R.A. Herriot, 2024.

James R.A. Herriot has asserted the moral right under the Copyright, Designs and Patents Act 1988 to be identified as the author of this work.

The views expressed in this work are solely those of the author, and do not necessarily reflect those of the publisher. The publisher hereby disclaims any responsibility for them.

This book is a work of non-fiction. Unless otherwise noted, the author and the publisher make no explicit guarantees as to the accuracy of the information included in this book and, in some cases, the names of people, places and organisations may have been altered to protect their privacy. All hyperlinks were believed to be live and correctly detailed at the time of publication.

This book may include references to organisations, feature films, television programmes, popular songs, musical bands, novels, reference books, and other creative works, the titles of which are trademarks and/or registered trademarks, and which are the intellectual properties of their respective copyright holders.

All rights reserved. No part of this publication may be reproduced, stored in a retrieval system, or transmitted, in any form or by any means, electronic, mechanical, photocopying, recording or otherwise, without the prior permission in writing of the publisher.

This book is sold subject to the condition that it shall not, by way of trade or otherwise, be lent, re-sold or hired out, or otherwise circulated without the publisher's prior consent in any form of binding or cover other than that in which it is published and without a similar condition including this condition being imposed on the subsequent purchaser.

A CIP catalogue record for this book is available from the British Library.

ISBN: 978-1-7394845-2-1

Typeset in Creato Display.

Printed and bound in Great Britain by IngramSpark, Chapter House, Pitfield, Kiln Farm, Milton Keynes, MK11 3LW, United Kingdom.

Cover artwork is Copyright © Callerton, all rights reserved.

Cover design and book design is Copyright © David Knaggs.

Author images are Copyright © James R.A. Herriot, all rights reserved.

Archive photography is sourced from Callerton's digital picture library archive unless otherwise stated in the Image Credits section, which forms an extension of this legal page. The copyrights of third parties are reserved. All third party imagery is used under the provision of Fair Use for the purposes of commentary and criticism. While every reasonable effort has been made to contact copyright holders and secure permission for all images reproduced in this work, we offer apologies for any instances in which this was not possible and for any inadvertent omissions.

INSIGHTS

TO KITCHEN DESIGN

40+ Years in the World of a
Design-led Kitchen Specialist

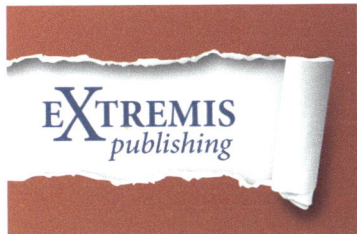

EXTREMIS
publishing

James R.A. Herriot

DESIGN DNA

Having not long stood down as
Chairman of 'Callerton', a kitchen
furniture manufacturing company
I founded with a friend some 40+ years ago:

**After 40+ years,
I offer an 'insight'
into the art of
crafting kitchens**

Enjoy

001 Rural Retreat

002 Conservatory to Garden Room

003 New Town Transformation

004 Diminutive Dimensions

005 Role Reversal

006 Modular Design

007 Pensilhaus Perfection

008 About Turn

009 Magnificent Milchester

010 Beautiful Barn

KITCHEN DESIGN SPECIALISTS

Venturing beyond my designs,
we explore the artistry of kitchen
specialists, showcasing timeless
creations and innovative reimagination.

**Great design
is timeless;
our diverse
kitchens are
a testament
to evolving
creativity over
15 years**

**Each kitchen
tells a unique
story, crafted by
specialists from
our National
Network**

106

011 Extreme Restoration

012 Island Ingenuity

013 Design Divergence

014 Poignant Project

015 Pièce de Résistance

016 Grand Design

017 Minimalist Marvel

018 Salutary Style

019 Party Central

020

CONTENTS

DESIGN DYNAMICS

Celebrating four decades in design, innovation meets inspiration as showrooms tell a tale of passion and precision.

021 Industrial Grace

022 Tranquil Dining

023 Urban Allure

024 Eclectic Luxe

025 Graceful Opulence

026 Sophisticated Form

027 Sublime Oasis

028 Modern Majesty

029 Timeless Grandeur

030 Refined Luxury

p194

RK-Tec LEGACY

RK-Tec Legacy: Celebrating 15 Years of Kitchen Excellence, Collaboration, and Design Innovation

031 blum

032 NEFF

033 FRANKE

034 SIEMENS

035 silestone

036 Cyncly

037 DEKTON

038 sensio

039 BOSCH

040 Callerton

p218

DESIGN
DN

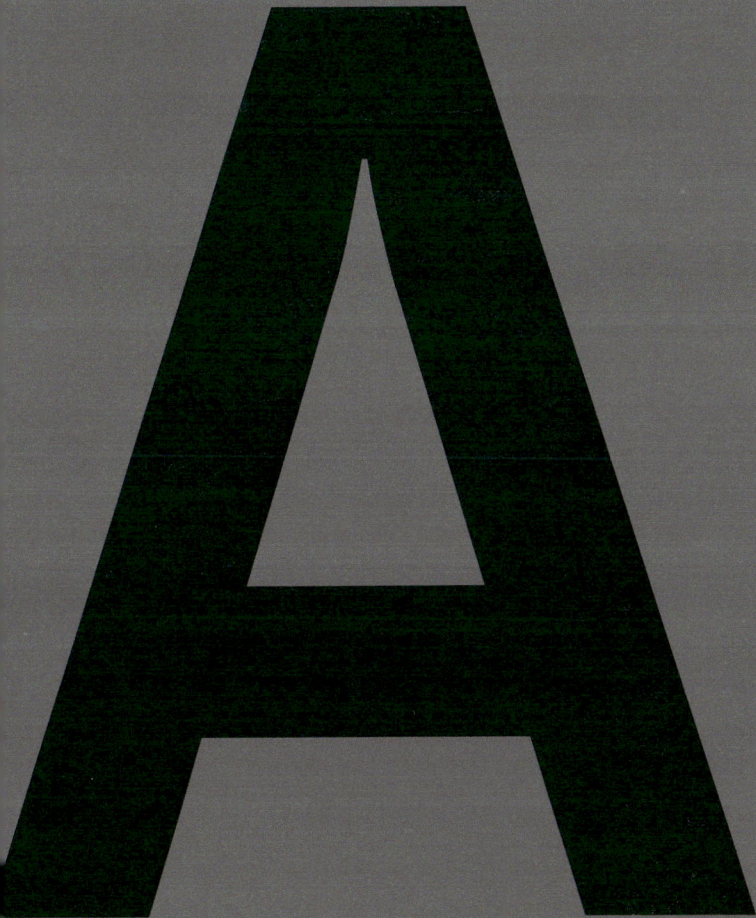

40 Years of Design Evolution

To those with an interest in Kitchen Design

Insights to Kitchen Design is an attempt to shine a light on 40+ years working in kitchen design. The design-led kitchen industry is a bit like a drug and one that's difficult to step away from. Involvement in the design and creation of projects that revolutionise the way clients live their lives is highly addictive, satisfying and runs through my veins.

Having not long stood down as Chairman of 'Callerton' a kitchen furniture manufacturing company I founded with a friend some 40+ years ago:

Having not long stood down as Chairman of 'Callerton', a kitchen furniture manufacturing company I founded with a friend some four decades ago, I was far from enamoured when my leaving present proved to be a pair of slippers. I was more than happy to step back from the day-to-day cut and thrust of running a business (after 40+ years) and to hand over to younger members of the team to ensure the long-term sustainability and success of our enterprise.

The issue arose in relation to kitchen design being my equivalent to Crosswords, Sudoku and Wordle – it's in my blood. I was/am most likely dyslectic, not something understood or recognised when I attended school many decades ago. What this fascinating spectrum provides me with is an ability to interpret a flat plan (in my head) via 3D and colour – I thrive on imagery and creativity.

After 40+ years, I offer an 'Insight' into the art of crafting kitchens

Crosswords, Sudoku and Wordle are a total anathema to me – but creating an exciting and innovative design presses all the right buttons and an absolute passion of mine. Hence my decision to provide an 'Insight' to kitchen design.

Insights to Kitchen Design incorporates a series of kitchen projects I and fellow Callerton colleagues have had involvement, from either a design or manufacturing perspective, and revisiting each of these and creating alternative (contrasting) designs based on the original footprint. Design evolves continuously – so a fresh look at each project with a new perspective and context.

To mark 40 years in designer kitchens I've raided Callerton's (the company I jointly founded) extensive archive/portfolio and picked out 20 which highlight the diverse and varied nature of each individual project. Alongside the 20 actual kitchens (with much assistance from colleagues) we've generated 2 contrasting alternative designs for each of these to highlight the multitude of options and possibilities available.

A further aspect of my role related to the development and creation of innovative showroom displays - 'Insights' incorporates a series of these to highlight the disparate nature of design.

My aim and intention being to provide an 'Insight' to a fascinating profession.

Enjoy

James R.A. Herriot

001
Rural Retreat

002
Conservatory to Garden Room

003
New Town Transformation

004
Diminutive Dimensions

005

Role Reversal

006

Modular Design

007

Passivhaus Perfection

008

About Turn

009

Magnificent Milchester

010

Beautiful Barn

RURAL RETREAT

A long narrow house with an outdated and inefficient kitchen at one end, separated from the dining room by a sitting room and hallway – not the most efficient of arrangements. Just one of various issues facing the owners of this rural property: no ground floor WC, no utility room, 2 front doors, lack of sunlight, decrepit central heating, and poor insulation.

Rural Retreat
2003

Project 001

Where does one start when you know the layout and facilities don't meet expectations? This enterprising young couple invited me to look at reconfiguring the design of their home to ensure their concept of a kitchen, living and breakfast room could be achieved. Additional items on their wish list included a standalone guest suite, utility room, ground floor WC, and a wine cellar. An added googly related to hosting up to 24 at a single table on the odd occasion.

Where does one start when you know the layout & facilities don't meet expectations

I believe it goes without saying that food and entertaining family and friends were an important requisite for my clients.

Working with clients to establish their aims, wishes, & criteria is the secret to a successful project

As you'll see, a radical makeover was called for if their many and varied requirements were to be met. Working with clients to establish their aims, wishes and criteria is the secret to a successful project. Also, in this case we had to ensure the reconfiguration of the house was in association with the new kitchen. You'd be amazed how often the kitchen is brought into the equation much later in proceedings – which can prove to be a grave and costly error.

The solution proved fairly radical: the decision being to rebuild much of the east end of the original building. This single storey structure incorporated a dilapidated pantile roof and the opportunity to reconfigure the layout. By adding a 2nd storey, a standalone guest suite was possible. Removal of a front door balanced the northern elevation. Changing the orientation and creating a ground floor WC, utility room and rear hallway answered other issues.

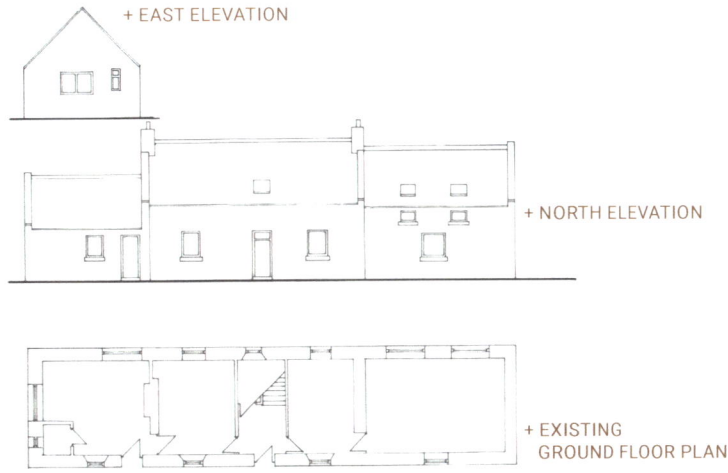

+ EAST ELEVATION

+ NORTH ELEVATION

+ EXISTING GROUND FLOOR PLAN

RADICAL SOLUTION

+ FIRST FIX COMPLETED AHEAD OF DECORATION & KITCHEN DELIVERY

Raising the original roofline to facilitate the guest suite enabled a glazed extension to be incorporated into the new ground floor formation. A major benefit, as the floor to ceiling glazing encapsulates spectacular views of the garden into the heart of the house. Removal of a large standalone chimney breast added 600mm in width to the sitting room/ breakfast room. Creating two archways from this area enabled kitchen, living and dining to be achieved.

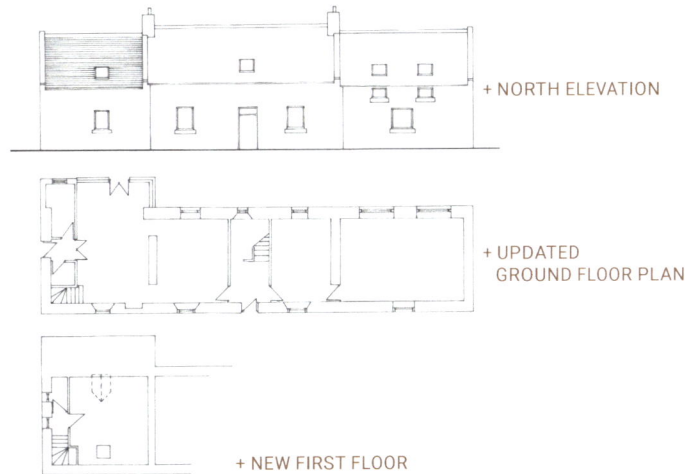

Expending time and effort on establishing what's required of the building in conjunction with the new kitchen made certain the overall layout and function came together and provided an all-encompassing solution.

+ NORTH ELEVATION

+ UPDATED GROUND FLOOR PLAN

+ NEW FIRST FLOOR

Designing a successful kitchen involves getting inside the head of my clients

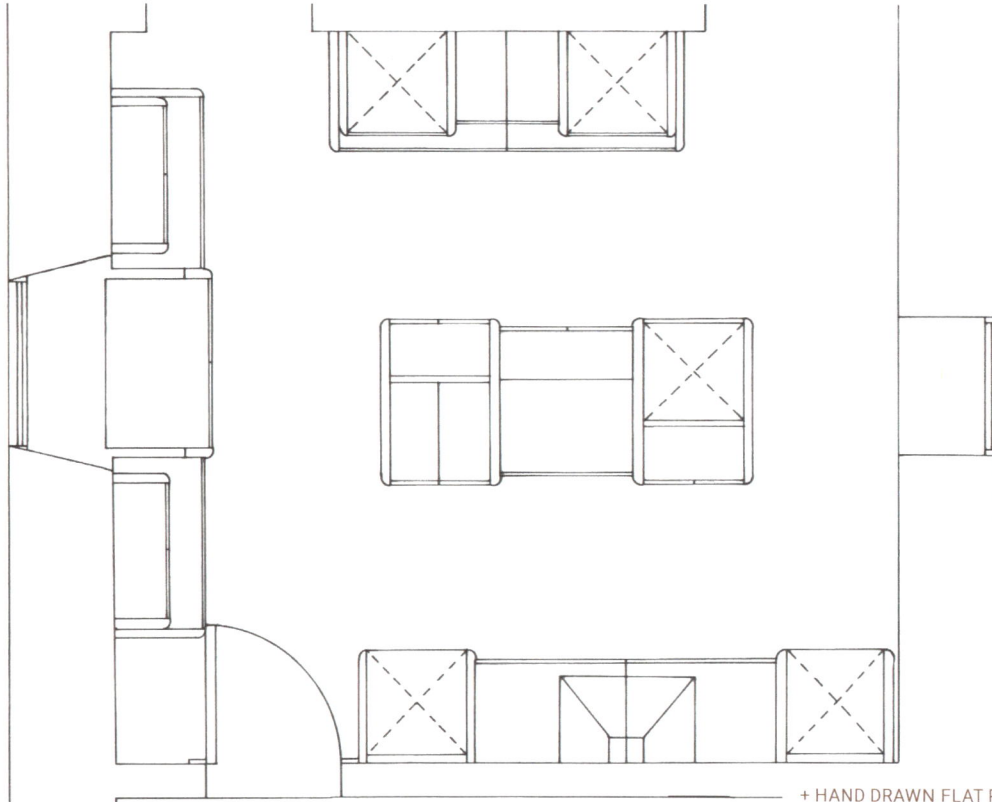

+ HAND DRAWN FLAT PLAN

Moving the kitchen to the original small sitting room resolved the issue of access to the dining room (now across the hall). The structural element which transforms the new kitchen relates to the incorporation of two archways leading to the breakfast/living area. These provide the illusion of connectivity and a single room. A further small alteration was to adjust the position of the door into the main hallway. This enabled a much improved kitchen layout.

Designing a successful kitchen involves getting inside the head of my clients and establishing their individual criteria. Callerton's 'Design Criteria Document' is a long-time essential. As previously established this had to be a cook's kitchen: family, friends, food, wine, and entertaining were all important aspects of this particular family's modus operandi.

Their appliance requirements ran to: two ovens, microwave, steam oven, electric and gas hob (hedge against power cuts), stylish extraction, dishwasher, good size fridge and separate freezer. A tap with a spray attachment and filtered water was deemed important, and preferably two separate sinks. Easily accessible drawers rather than cupboards (no corner cabinetry). A centre island with lots of preparation space. Appliances, where possible, at a height (due to a back issue). A sound system to be incorporated. Good lighting, and adaptable to suit the mood.

Hopefully this provides an insight to understanding the needs and requirements of my clients. To which I must add the furniture and design to be timeless (this to be a one-off exercise). Timber furniture, stand-out handles, glazed cabinetry, quartz work surfaces, design inspired Amtico floor, and elegant ceiling cornice detail were all to be incorporated.

I leave you to decide whether the brief was fulfilled: - first via the plans, then a recent photo shoot of the project. I should add that the kitchen is approaching 20 years old – testament to 'Timeless Design'. As an addendum, the final image demonstrates the recently-installed 'Wine Cellar' - the original budget hadn't run to the incorporation of this.

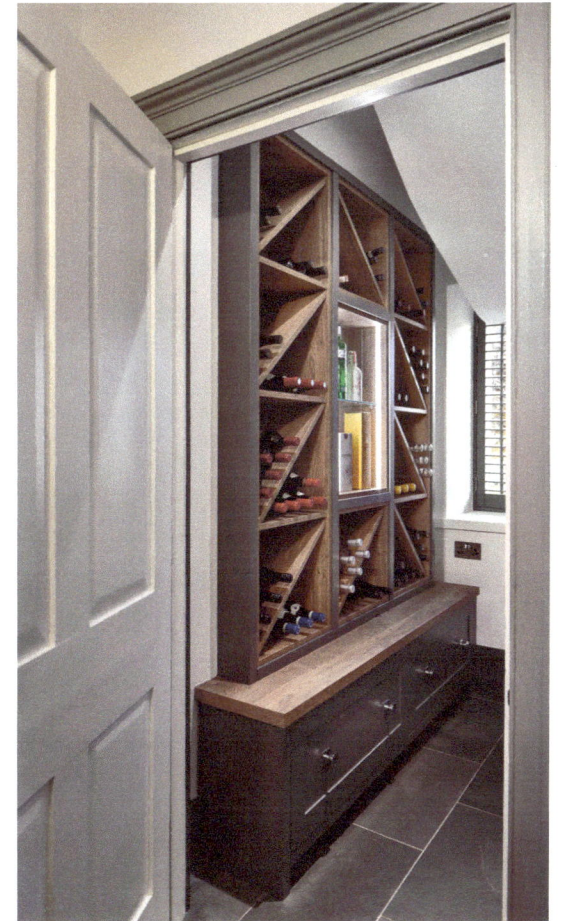

Rural Retreat
Alternative 1
Project 001

Inspiration

CLASSIC REVITALISATION:
A Fusion of Contrasting Colours & Elements

A totally different look, vibe and function via incorporation of painted furniture and oak ingredients. Plus a breakfast bar integrated within the island, practicality of a bi-fold butler's pantry, a dresser to display treasured items, traditional Belfast sink, combination of wood and quartz worksurfaces. An apt demonstration of the many diverse options available within the World of Designer Kitchens.

Park Green
Smooth
Flat Painted

Cathcart
Smooth
Flat Painted

Pure
Mink
Stained Oak

Orphic
Scuro Oak
Chalet

Natural
Carini Walnut
Cabinets

Orphic
Kiruna Grigio
Artstone

Onyx
Grey
Cabinets

Monza
Matt
Frost White

Orphic
Tigerwood
Nero

Orphic
Scuro Oak
Chalet

Rural Retreat
Alternative 2
Project 001

Inspiration

SLEEK TRANSITION:
Combination of Industrial, Timber, Matt & Stone Elements

A contrast to the incumbent kitchen utilising a variety of high tech materials as well as accommodating adaptions to both functionality and style. Once more a breakfast bar included within the island – with simpler, cleaner lines. A tall bank housing ovens and refrigeration - includes illuminated open shelving to soften the look. Sleek glazed wall cabinetry is at variance with the prior Shaker concept.

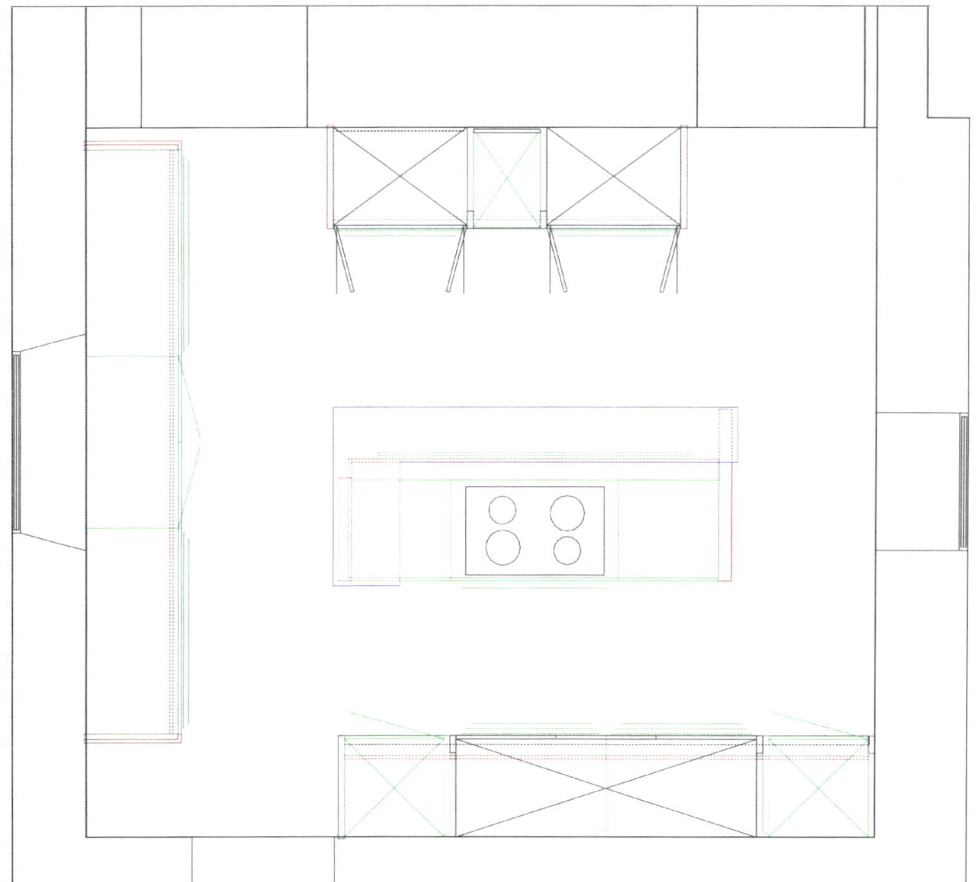

Conservatory to Garden Room

An invitation a decade ago to a meeting with the then Housing Minster, alongside stalwarts of the Self Build market, by chance led to Callerton's long-term and fruitful involvement with Potton's innovative Show Centre and Self Build Academy at St Neots (Cambridgeshire), which consists of five contrasting and fascinating show-houses.

The first kitchen project our Design Team were invited to participate in related to their traditional Gransden show home. This was originally constructed 30 or so years ago, and was in need of a makeover. The Gransden's conservatory proved to be an issue: it was too hot in summer and too cold in winter. The layout of the house was also deemed to hark back to an earlier era and required an update to incorporate the trend towards a more open-plan kitchen, living and dining area.

Potton had previously made the decision to remove the existing conservatory, to be replaced with a highly insulated Garden Room to house the kitchen. As with any conversion project, people may have a vested interest in the original layout and feel loath to stray far from this. I understand such thinking, as it often relates to history and memories. This project encountered those who wished to retain more of the original layout — but others more open to change.

This is where the benefits of CAD (Computer Aided Design) come into their own. A discussion as to what's possible can often lead to a polarisation of views. Each individual's ability to visualise the design options and possibilities without the benefit of 3D CAD imagery will differ. Words, and an ability to interpret a design without imagery, are likely to lead to miscommunication. Hence, as per 40+ years of experience, the first aspect relates to identifying the 'Design Criteria'.

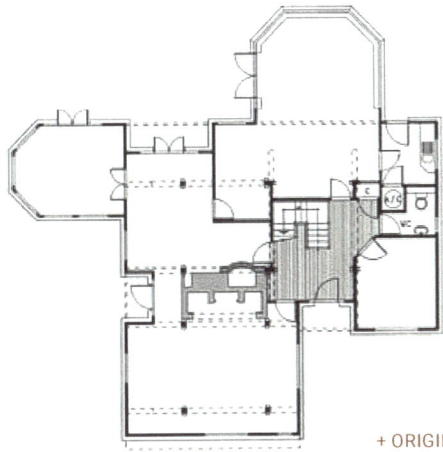

+ ORIGINAL PLAN WITH CONSERVATORY

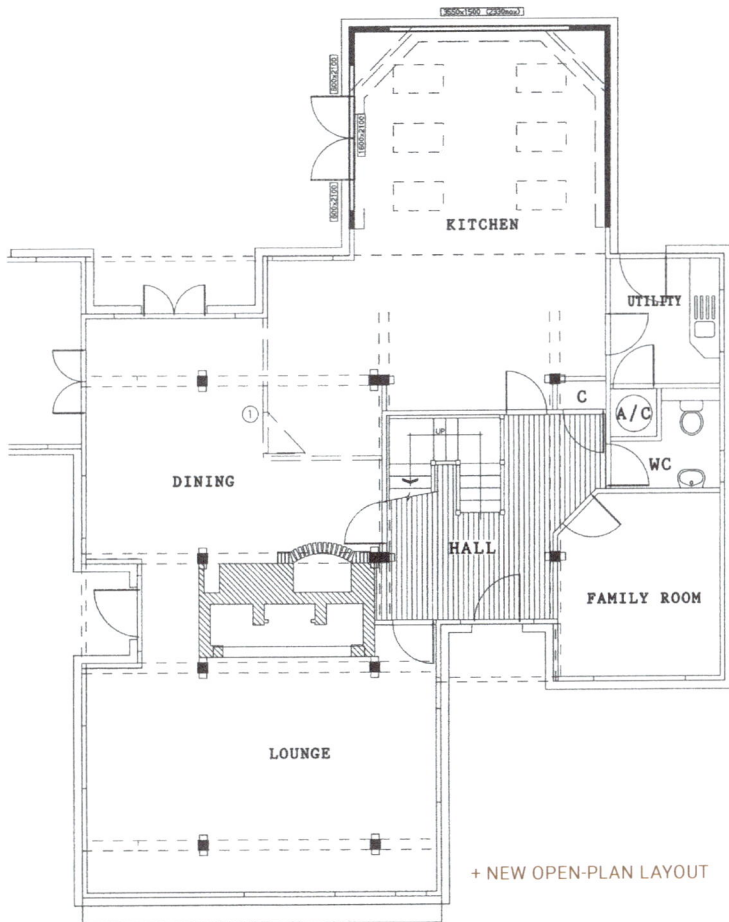

+ NEW OPEN-PLAN LAYOUT

What are the aims and ambitions for your particular project? Establishing these with your Kitchen Design Specialist ensures they are in a position to interpret such into your 'Dream Project'. Spending time identifying your likes, dislikes and wishes in advance of creating a design; a process well worth all the effort and energy. This project was no different.

A contrast in style was a major aim – anyone previously visiting the Gransden was to be wowed by the transformation. Unusually, it also had to be capable of catering for large groups of individuals attending Self Build Academy seminars – not an everyday kitchen requirement. Also, the hosting of high-end cookery demonstrations and dining events were also a consideration.

The plans of the original house layout, including the conservatory, identify the main lounge area plus the separate secondary sitting room, with the glazed dining area leading off this. Much discussion was had in relation to removing the wall between the existing kitchen and the secondary sitting room (my own preference), but this decision was not unanimously shared with all the Team at Potton – hence our offer to produce a full set of CAD imagery incorporating the removal of this.

As can be deduced from the CAD imagery, removal of the wall transforms the space and creates that open-plan element: an aspect of the original design brief. Building a brand new Potton home involves high levels of insulation - an important characteristic of open-plan living. Having established the change in the ground floor layout, as well as the dimensions and detail of the new Garden Room, work commenced on the kitchen design.

+ PREVIOUS KITCHEN & CONSERVATORY

+ KITCHEN PLAN & CAD RENDER

+ DOWNDRAFT VENTILATION COMPLETED DURING BUILDING WORK

An exciting kitchen can be achieved without breaking the bank

A further aspect of the original design brief related to the new kitchen having impact - but the budget was not infinite. It was to demonstrate that an exciting kitchen can be achieved without breaking the bank. A flat panel contemporary door, in the main, is less expensive than a five-part traditional door. The wise utilisation of materials and finishes can majorly impact on overall cost – hence the choices made, and the decision to utilise elements of a Crossover/Hybrid design.

As will be demonstrated in the alternative kitchen designs for the Gransden, beauty and design are very much in the eye of the beholder. Each individual will have their own preferences and needs: from high tech Contemporary to Traditional Classic, and a myriad of options in-between. Callerton's Design Team utilise the Gransden for educational purposes, and the following pages highlight two diverse CAD designs sourced from their training programme.

I leave you with imagery from the project, as well as photography of the nine year old design. This has stood the test of time, and has been well received by the many visitors to Potton's Show Centre. The Centre is open to the public, and if you're in the market for a self build project or a new kitchen then I can highly recommend a visit.

+ FIRST FIX & DECORATION COMPLETED AHEAD OF KITCHEN DELIVERY

Pure
Blue Grey
Stained Oak

Onyx
Grey
Cabinets

Monza
Matt Graphite

Special
Smooth
Flat Painted

Brass Effect
Laminate

Conservatory to Garden Room

Alternative 1

Inspiration

MULTI-GENERATIONAL:
The Benefits of Design
with Longevity

Over a lifetime how many times does one
bend down to insert or remove something from
a drawer, cupboard or appliance? If via analysis
of ease of access you minimise such - imagine
the long-term benefits. This design also relates
to those with health conditions or impairments.
Many years ago, I had the privilege of meeting
an extraordinary woman who, despite being
impacted by Thalidomide, skilfully adapted by
using multiple levels to fulfil specific tasks, setting
a remarkable example of resilience and ingenuity.

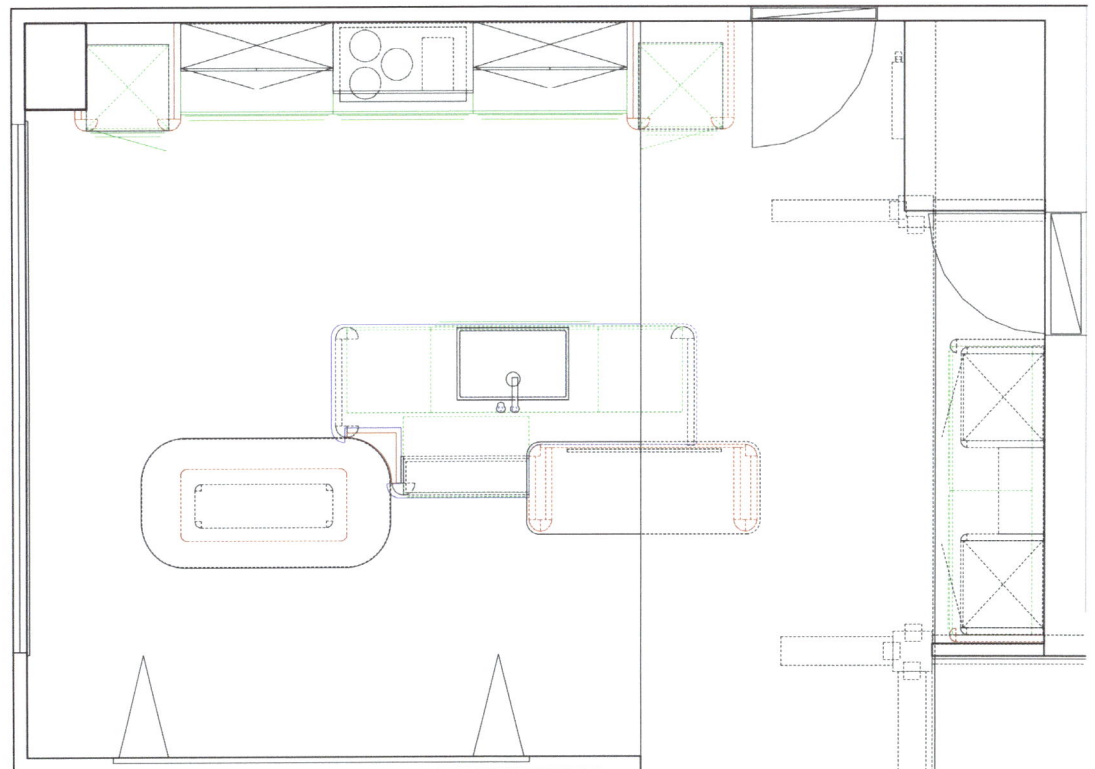

Conservatory to Garden Room

Alternative 2

Inspiration

FLOATING FURNITURE:
False Walls & Hidden Depths in a Minimalist Contemporary Design Concept

The illusion created via the incorporation of false walls disguising the depth of the furniture provides a different dimension to the prior alternative design. The tall floating modules accommodate fridge and freezer, ovens and storage, practical pocket doored cabinetry, plus matching TV bank. The island incorporates a breakfast bar, wine and conventional storage, open shelving and lots of work-surface.

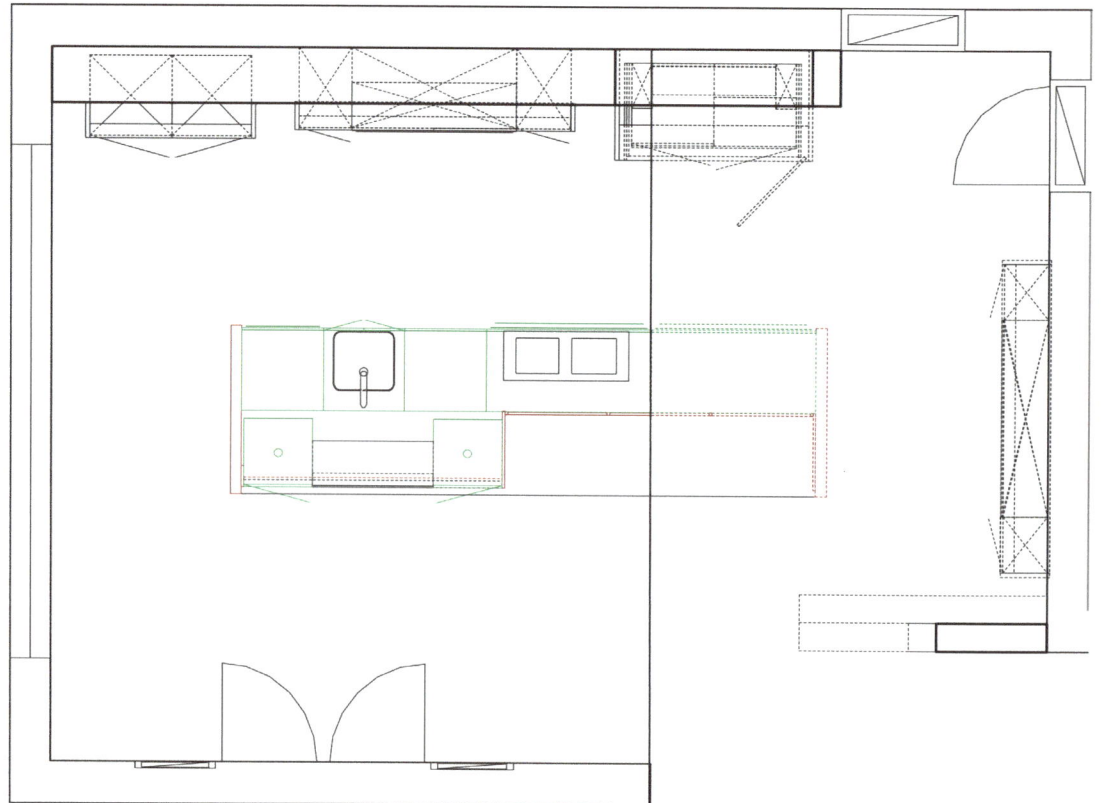

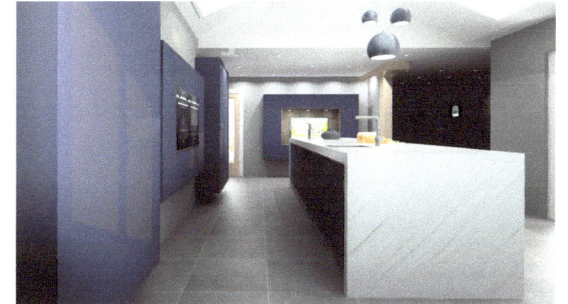

Monza
Matt Indigo

Natural
Carini Walnut
Cabinets

Abstract
Natural Carini
Walnut

Grey Tint
Mirror

New Town

Transformation

This humble mid-terraced house is a testament to working within a budget, yet delivering beyond expectations

This particular project debunks the myth 'Exciting, Design Inspired Kitchens': the preserve of those with a high-end property and budget. Cramlington New Town dates back to the 1960s, and is a satellite of Newcastle-upon-Tyne. The architecture of the time lacks imagination; the owner of this modest '60s terraced house recognised it was unlikely to win awards. But nonetheless, it was her family home and community, and hence the property was extremely meaningful and significant.

As a designer it's important to establish budget parameters – there's no sense in creating a masterpiece way beyond the means of your client. This only leads to disappointment for all concerned. This humble mid-terraced house is a perfect example of working within a budget, but delivering way beyond the client's expectations. It also highlights what can be achieved within a constrained footprint. Such projects are as equally satisfying to resolve as any high-end proposition.

I often liken kitchen design to the board game 'Snakes & Ladders'. This is never more significant than dealing with smaller kitchens and attempting to ensure that all of the client's many wishes, aims and dreams can be attained. The available space/size tends to restrict ambitions for a centre island, American fridge/freezer, separate table, etc.

The old adage that 'you can't fit a Quart into a Pint Pot' relates well to more diminutive kitchens – inevitably there will have to be compromises. On the face of it, this particular project would at first glance appear to be very much of this ilk, as the imagery and plan of the original layout helps to demonstrate. As an avid cookery aficionado and someone who likes to have friends and family round for coffee and meals, it's easy to see why my client was unhappy with retaining the existing layout.

One interesting point: my client previously had another company come and look at updating the kitchen. Having explained how nothing in the kitchen worked for her – a totally impractical layout for someone who loves to cook, with no preparation space, lack of storage, not enough ovens, no opportunity to have others in the kitchen, etc. – their solution was to replace everything virtually as was, but in a different style. This led to total disillusionment on my client's part.

Hence, as a family friend, I was approached to take a look and see if I could assist. As ever, my initial procedure is to establish the design criteria – first and foremost, to get inside a client's head and determine what they wish to achieve from a new kitchen. Having taken dimensions, detail and photos of the existing kitchen, I left a copy of our 'Design Criteria Document' which probes for likes and dislikes, as well as more specific detail with reference to all the many areas involved.

The answers were telling, and explained dissatisfaction with the current arrangement. Cold and draughts were a major issue (unsuitable for prolonged periods), and they needed space for two ovens, warming drawer, coffee machine (since retiring now a part time barista at the local community farm shop), and a large fridge and freezer (they cooked and baked for countless others). There was not enough preparation space or storage, the washing machine/laundry and C/H boiler in the kitchen was an issue, and there were other issues.

Hopefully this provides an insight into generating a design brief before getting out the drawing board. Establishing a rapport with clients and coaxing out of them as much information and detail as possible helps in the process of creating a design that will truly fulfil their expectations. My client's efforts in this instance was of great benefit.

As an avid cookery aficionado, it's easy to see why my client was unhappy with retaining the existing layout

+ PRIOR TO DEVELOPMENT

"Have you got the right drawings? Is that my kitchen?"

The site survey established the original kitchen was even smaller (there had been a separate utility room); hence the cold and draughts (this floor was uninsulated and open to the elements). Also, the door from the garage was funnelling cold air into the kitchen; the external door and windows were highly inefficient. The ambience of a kitchen an important element.

Other issues gleaned from the site survey included two solid structural pillars to either side of the room (the original divide of kitchen and utility), a further issue being a ceiling bulkhead encroaching into the kitchen from the stairwell.

I leave you to peruse the CAD imagery of my design, which – as you'll see – is extremely close to the finished article. The secret to the design being the creation of a utility/laundry room in the garage, removing the wall between the living-room and lounge/dining area, altering the configuration of the doors and windows, plus the addition of insulation.

The comment when presenting the design and CAD imagery – "Have you got the right drawings? Is that my kitchen?" – says it all. I'm delighted to report that I've one happy and satisfied client. "It has changed the way I live," was a further comment.

+ ROOM DIMENSIONS FROM SITE SURVEY

+ CAD DESIGN USED DURING DESIGN PROCESS

New Town Transformation
Alternative 1
Project 003

Inspiration

PASTEL TONES:
From High Tech Contemporary to a Crossover/Hybrid

An interesting and contrasting proposition to the original utilising a combination of Shaker (handle and handless elements) and contemporary flat panelled doors in contrasting pastel colours. Also a change of layout with a table rather than breakfast bar and the addition of a butler's pantry. Individual client's needs and requirements invariably differ – hence an illustration of diverse tastes.

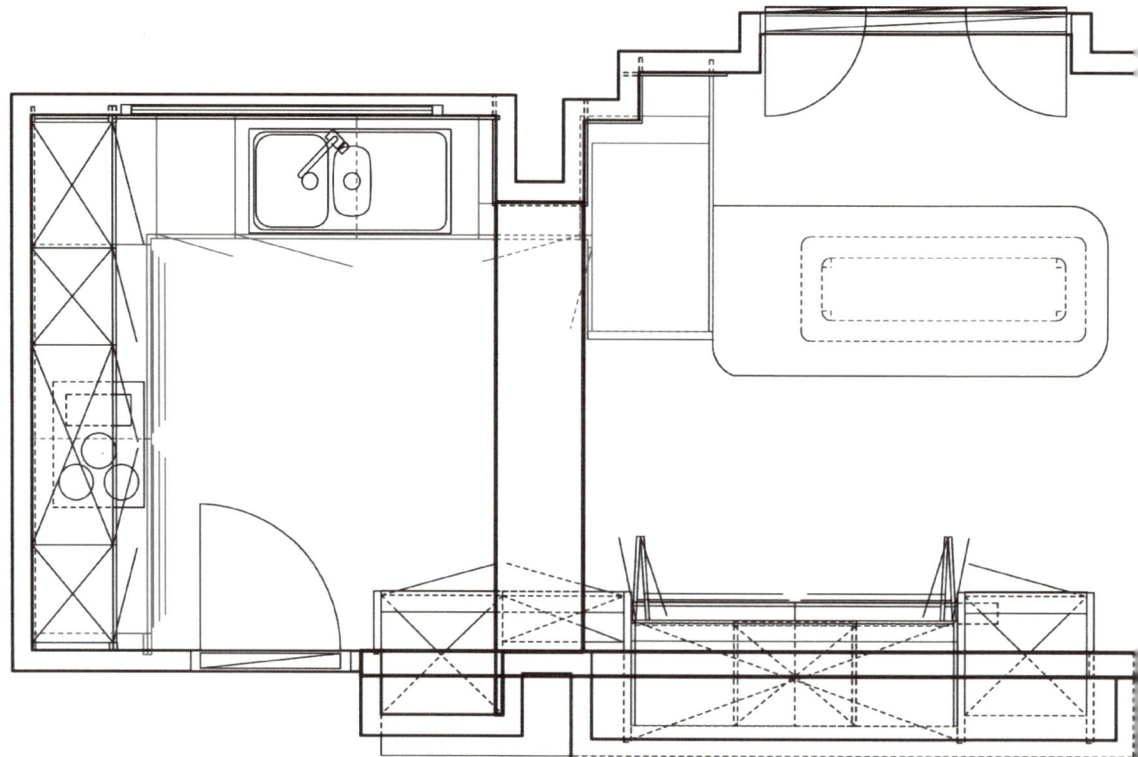

Special
Smooth
Flat Painted

Floret
Smooth
Flat Painted

Aluminium
Effect
Profile

Natural
Hamilton Oak
Cabinets

Orphic
Aged Oak
Grigio

Onyx
Grey
Cabinets

Abstract Expressions
Anthracite
Mountain Larch

Abstract Expressions
White Halifax
Oak

Brass
Effect
Profile

New Town Transformation
Alternative 2
Project 003

Inspiration

SUBTLE BUT STYLISH:
Aspects & Echoes
with a Contrasting
Dynamic

This project plagiarises elements of the previous two but with a number of subtle but effective additions. The style and colours are more towards the contemporary but augmented by open/dresser shelving in the centre of the tall bank which adds depth, alongside the open shelf combination within the wall cabinetry. Extended base cabinetry minus plinth adds a further touch.

DIMINUTIVE
DIMENSIONS

Dealing with a project when your clients reside in New York adds an extra dimension of challenge. An interesting young couple were on secondment to the States for two years – one with the UN, the other a Sotherby's fine wine specialist. Their abode in Manhattan was a diminutive (shoe-box) apartment on the 32nd floor of a skyscraper. For the duration of their time in New York, they rented out their equally compact one bedroom 1970s terraced house in Peckham (London).

Diminutive Dimensions
2019
Project 004

This project was pre-COVID and before the Global Pandemic, so it was an early lesson in working remotely via on-line documentation and video conferences. As can be deduced from the original flat plan and imagery, the house was in need of a complete make-over and transformation. The total ground floor area was less than 30 square metres, consisting of a hall, living room, kitchen, corridor and small backyard which was to be retained, hence no possibility of extending the footprint.

The more constrained the space, the more difficult it tends to be to satisfy your clients many wishes and desires for their project. A perfect example was that this young couple had a string of requests: a breakfast bar, separate table for six, two ovens, fridge and freezer, over-sized hob, large sink, dishwasher, effective extraction, and plenty of storage and preparation space were all important. As you may have deduced, they were avid cooks and entertainers.

In addition, the lady of the house had always wanted an electric piano, while her hubby lusted after a wine cooler. None of these on their own were an individual issue, but given the extremely limited space when including a settee, coffee table, two armchairs and bookcase, things became a little more tricky. Add in the desire for a second bedroom, and the scope of this project became even more complex – especially when the budget was restricted to a finite amount.

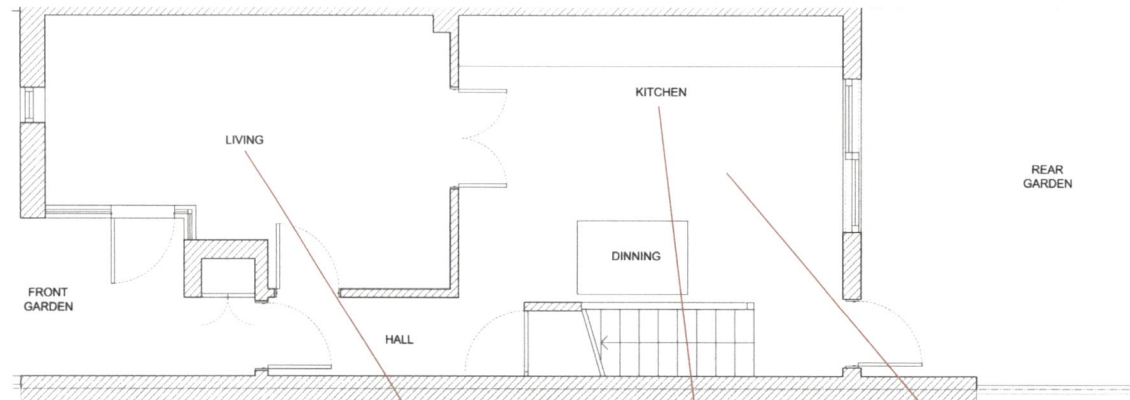

The house was in need of a complete make-over & transformation

+ EXISTING LAYOUT

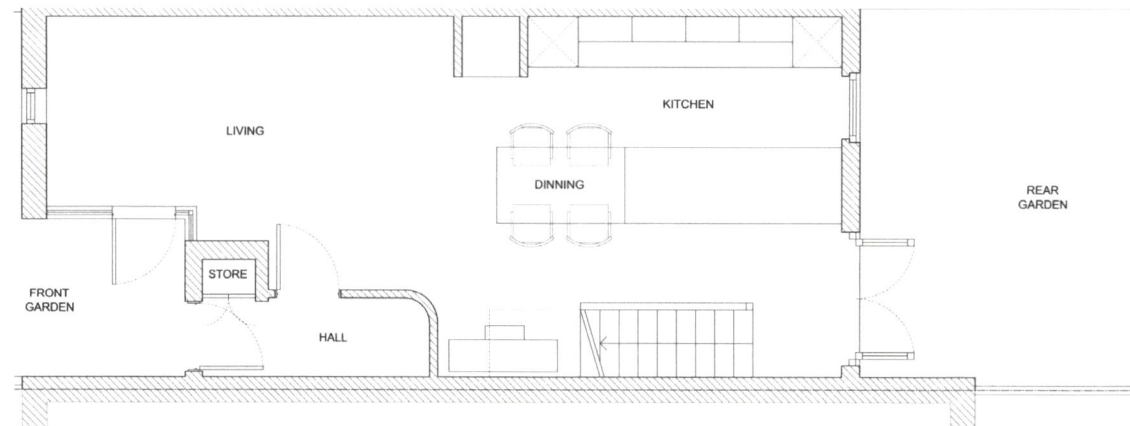

+ NEW OPEN-PLAN DESIGN

New York
Living in Peckham

New York life had inspired them in relation to creating the equivalent of Manhattan loft-living in Peckham. As a designer it is useful to understand as much about your client's aims, wishes and desires in advance as is possible. This enterprising young pair were surprisingly clear on these, but with no concept as to how any of this was to be attained.

The secret of limited space is to create the illusion that it is greater than the physical dimensions. In this instance, there was no option to utilise the front elevation – this being immediately onto the street. But the rear elevation and incorporation of the backyard were a possibility. The overall footprint, length and width were sacrosanct and set in stone.

The obvious solution was to remove the internal walls and create one large open space. The structure of the house, having originally been a council development, was unclear and required the expertise of a structural engineer to ensure this was possible and met building regulations. Having established such then opened up new opportunities.

To trick the eye, incorporation of a transformed backyard to an enclosed paved patio area into the kitchen provided the illusion of extra depth and light. This was achieved by installing patio doors and a full length fixed-light window. Moving the front door forward added extra space to the entrance hall, and incorporation of a curved wall diverts the eye from the many straight lines. Simple alterations, but they all make a difference in relation to both storage and looks.

+ CAD IMAGES USED DURING DESIGN PROCESS

On returning from New York: "Is this really our house?!"

The power of transformative design

Running an oak floor front to back added to the illusion of size. The colour palette in a conversion such as this becomes important, as natural light was restricted to the two external walls. Artificial lighting as and when the sun goes down was another significant aspect. The decision to incorporate a crossover/hybrid kitchen, with a combination of Shaker painted with bronze handles and matt handleless contemporary furniture, makes a dramatic statement.

An important issue related to the siting of the combination washer/dryer: there was no room in the kitchen, entrance hall or first floor. This was dealt with by its concealment in a cupboard below the stairs. As you will have seen from the CAD drawings and in the final photography, a home was found for the piano, and two small wine coolers were incorporated into the breakfast-bar.

The seamless Corian work surfaces in a light veined finish add to the combination of effects, and all come together to make the kitchen appear more spacious than seems possible given the limited physical dimensions. The bulkhead housing the in-built extraction above the central peninsular adds a further architectural element to the kitchen.

As to whether or not the kitchen fulfilled the clients criteria and aspirations is demonstrated by their reaction on first viewing the completed project on returning from New York: "Is this really our house?!"

Diminutive Dimensions
Alternative 1
Project 004

Inspiration

NEW-FANGLED FASHION: Sets the Scene for a Divergent Ambiance

A truly modern and divergent take from the actual hybrid kitchen. Simple clean-cut lines compliment the practical layout – form and function come together as one. Given the diminutive dimensions the peninsular and galley nature make use of every last inch (mm). A thought provoking design highlighting the vast and broad range of possibilities and options available to prospective clients.

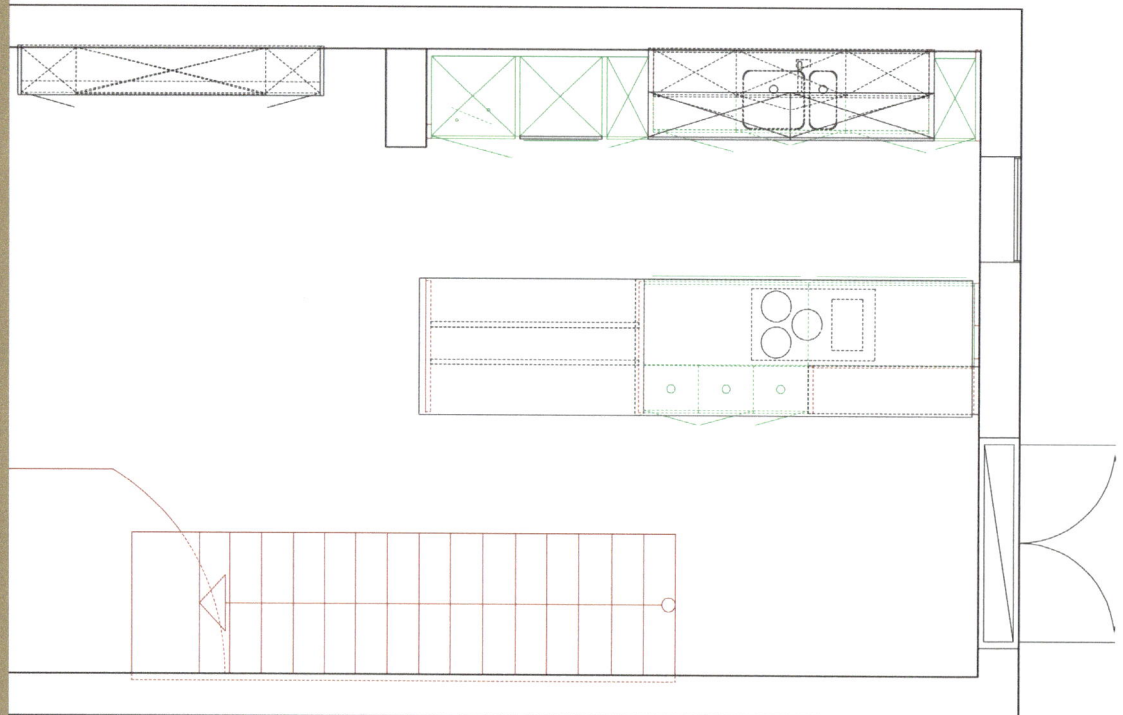

Inky Green
Grain Painted

Onyx
Grey
Cabinets

Abstract
Expressions
Anthracite
Fabric Metal

Black
Mirrored
Glass

**Pure
Dark Grey
Stained Oak**

**Onyx
Grey
Cabinets**

**English White
Smooth
Flat Painted**

**Satin
Nickel**

**Rubbed
Bronze**

Diminutive Dimensions
Alternative 2
Project 004

Inspiration

OPEN SESAME:
An Enlightening but
Apt Magical Phrase

The design concept allies well to the title
and the opening up of opportunities and
the utilisation of what are constrained
dimensions. A highly effective crossover
design incorporating both modern and
classic elements. The treatment to the
rear of the peninsular, with framed open
shelving and the contrasting glazed
cabinetry in the wet area, alongside
modern interventions - deserve mention.

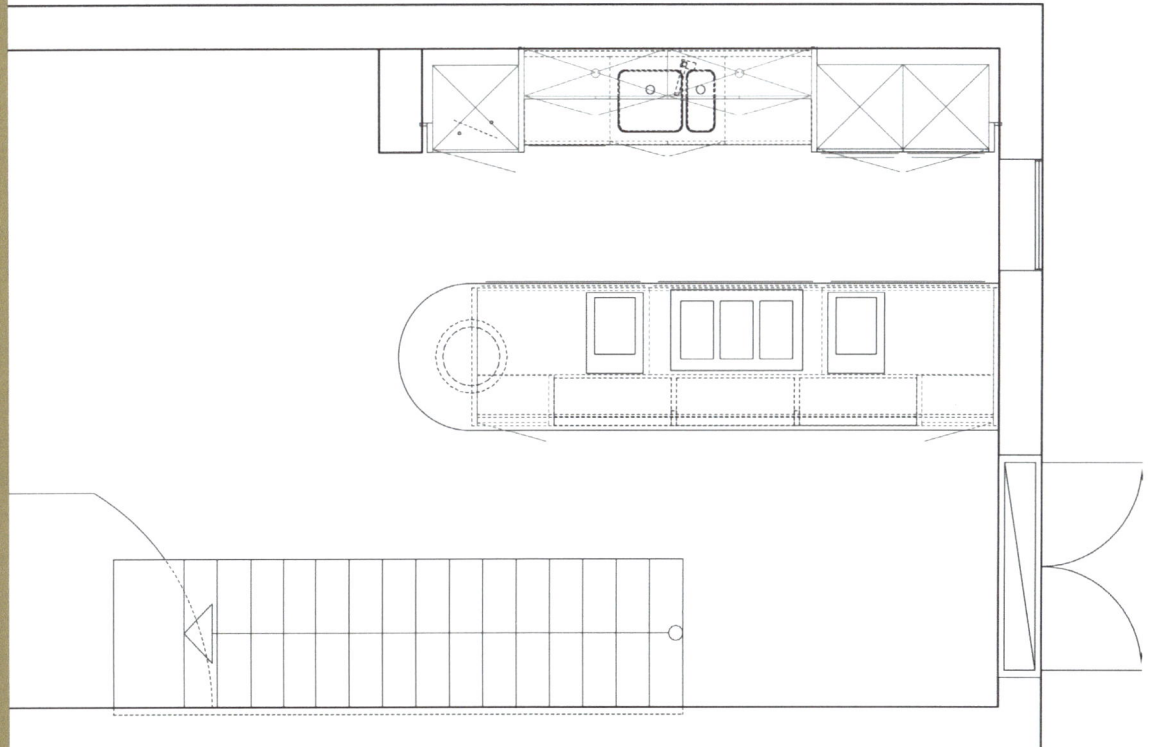

ROLE REVERSAL

I view my role in creating a client's 'Dream Kitchen' as being one that examines all options & possibilities. Establishing their aims, wishes and desires for such is the crucial initial step. But as per this particular project, there is often no way to fulfil the many requirements without a radical rethink in relation to reconfiguring or repurposing the layout of the property.

Role Reversal
2020
Project 005

This property belonged to a young professional couple with two children, aged 7 and 10. Their ambition was for the project to provide combined kitchen, living and dining around which the whole family could be actively involved and enjoy. As the original plans of the house ably demonstrate, this was not going to be achieved by retaining the kitchen in its original location.

This characterful traditional stone-built house looked quaint from the outside, but an earlier conversion placed the kitchen to the rear and guest bedroom suite adjacent to the front door. Adding to this, the original kitchen lacked any view or sunlight as it looked immediately onto a steep gradient with no possibility of extending outward. An added issue was the back door which led immediately into the kitchen, making the room cold and draughty.

Making a house perform and flow relates to ensuring that everything is in the right place. The kitchen was at the back of the property, away from the living accommodation – not ideal. Add in the guest bedroom suite (bedroom and bathroom) immediately off the hall and opposite the living area, and this was not how you would plan things given a blank sheet of paper.

The original kitchen lacked any view or sunlight as it looked immediately onto a steep gradient with no possibility of extending outward

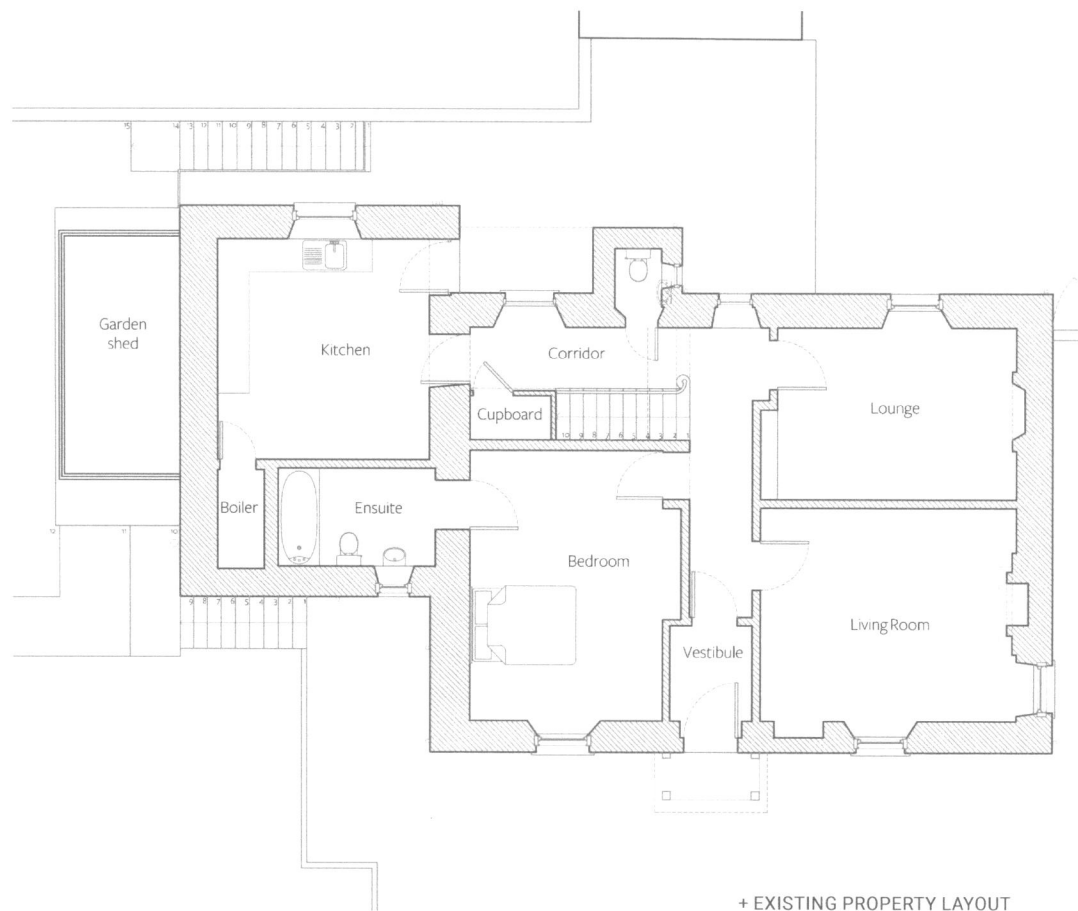

+ EXISTING PROPERTY LAYOUT

When reconfiguring an existing property, it's important to look at the orientation regards sunlight and views. As in this case, why provide these advantages to a guest bedroom suite (utilised infrequently and mainly overnight) when the original kitchen possessed no such benefits. This particular project was one that would profit from repurposing the ground floor layout to make it more user-friendly, efficient and practical.

I've rather put the cart before the horse in that, prior to establishing all of the above, I first worked with my clients as to their requirements and criteria for their new kitchen. Kitchen, living and dining were all firmly on the agenda. But what about cooking/kitchen necessities in relation to appliances, sinks, taps, work surfaces, storage, layout, etc.? As ever, Callerton's trusty 'Design Criteria' document assisted in expanding my knowledge as to all of their various aspirations.

The list was extensive: Shaker painted furniture with stand-out handles, a centre-island, breakfast bar for four, a butler's pantry, bookcase, quartz work surfaces, two ovens, a microwave, a large induction hob, efficient extraction, fridge/freezer, dishwasher, double Belfast sink, brass tap, fancy radiator, mood lighting. Establishing this information makes my job in interpreting such into the kitchen of their dreams a much simpler process – the more information and detail, the better.

Kitchen, Living & Dining

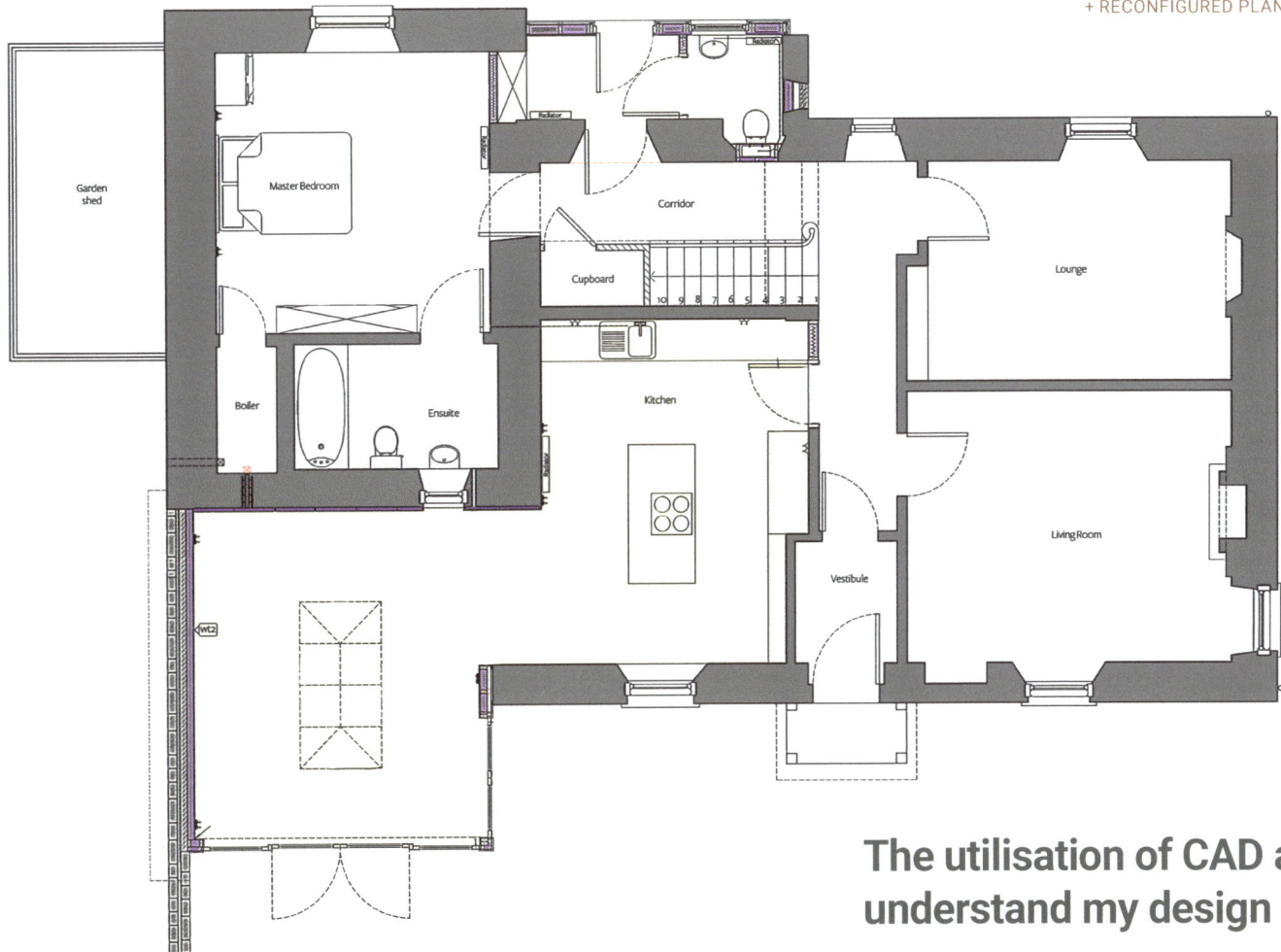

Garden shed

Master Bedroom

Corridor

Cupboard

Boiler

Ensuite

Kitchen

Lounge

Living Room

Vestibule

My initial thoughts related to a total role reversal: move the guest bedroom suite to the site of the current kitchen, and then house the new kitchen in the guest bedroom. Potentially the ensuite could be retained by repositioning the doorway. If this all proved possible, the living and dining elements of the new kitchen could be generated by building a new contemporary glazed extension. So the first step was to establish whether the kitchen element could work.

As always, the utilisation of CAD (computer aided design) assists clients to understand my design thoughts. As you can see, the imagery demonstrates that by moving the position of the door into the kitchen, blocking up the existing door way to the ensuite bathroom via incorporation of a bookcase, and knocking a large opening through the adjacent wall to a new contemporary extension, the kitchen could work within the confines of the existing guest bedroom.

The utilisation of CAD assists clients to understand my design thoughts

An architect was engaged at this point, as the house is situated in a conservation area on the outskirts of Edinburgh. Their plan of the revamped ground floor layout demonstrates how the role reversal works, and indicates the incorporation of the new living/dining extension. The architects handled the gaining of planning permission and building regulations, as well as putting the project out to tender. A building contractor was then appointed, and the project commenced.

The revamped ground floor layout demonstrates how the role reversal works, & indicates the incorporation of the new living/dining extension

To cut a long and convoluted story short, the project began prior to Christmas, just before the Pandemic hit. Thus my clients and their project were heavily impacted by Government Lockdowns, the need to work remotely, home-schooling two children, difficulty in sourcing materials, and trades in Scotland being banned from working on site. They were put through the mill.

All's well that ends well, however, as is demonstrated by the photography of the finished article.

Orphic
Kiruna Grigio
Artstone

Onyx
Grey
Cabinets

Monza
Matt
Frost White

Orphic
Aged Oak
Grigio

Grey Tint
Mirror

Role Reversal
Alternative 1
Project 005

COUNTERINTUITIVE:
The Total Opposite to Original Thoughts

The creation of a Dream Kitchen benefits from examining the vast range of possible alternatives and opportunities – in this instance a total Role Reversal. Which can also relate to looks and style – every client is an individual with their own tastes and requirements hence the reason to dissect what is possible. This well represented by the alternative layout to the original - with clean cut modern lines.

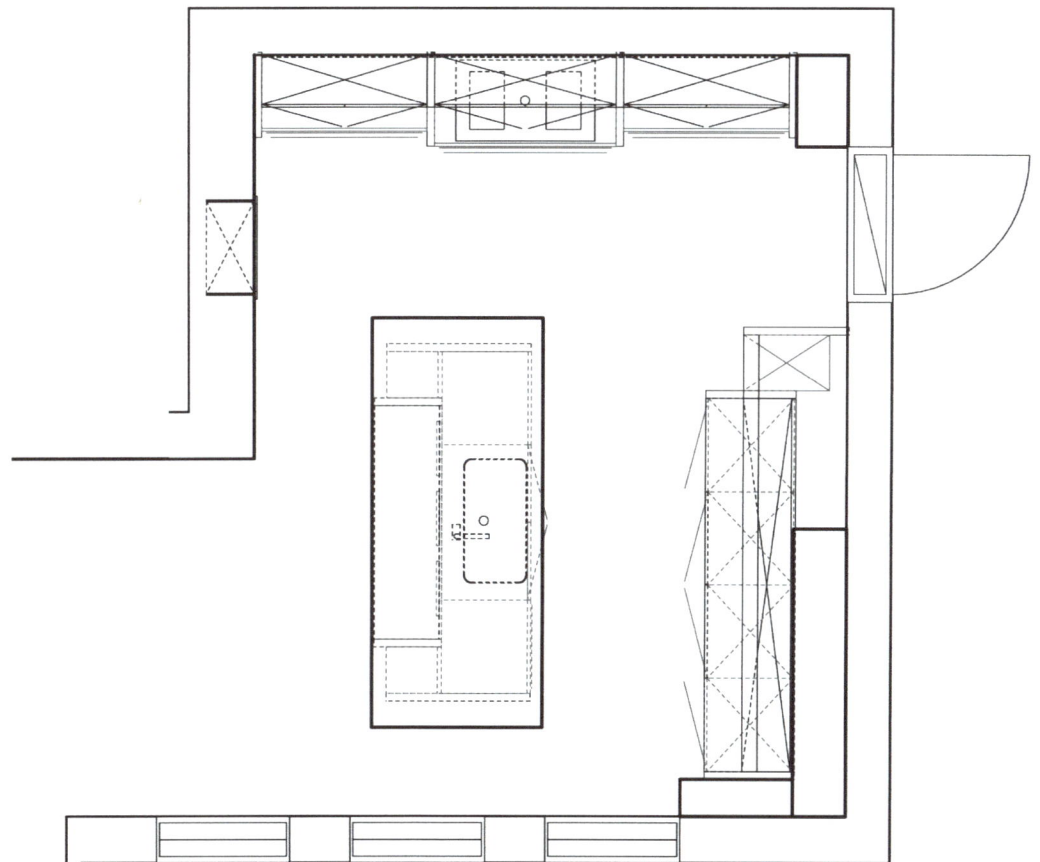

Role Reversal
Alternative 2
Project 005

Inspiration

BALANCE, SYMMETRY & PERSPECTIVE:
Vital Elements in Creative Design

The utilisation of open cabinetry, the breaking back and forward as well as alterations to height - adds a further dimension to this interesting alternative. The eclectic combination of modern timber effects with industrial concrete textures generates a juxtaposition with the prior plain matt example. An important element of any kitchen is lighting – even more so when associated with open cabinets.

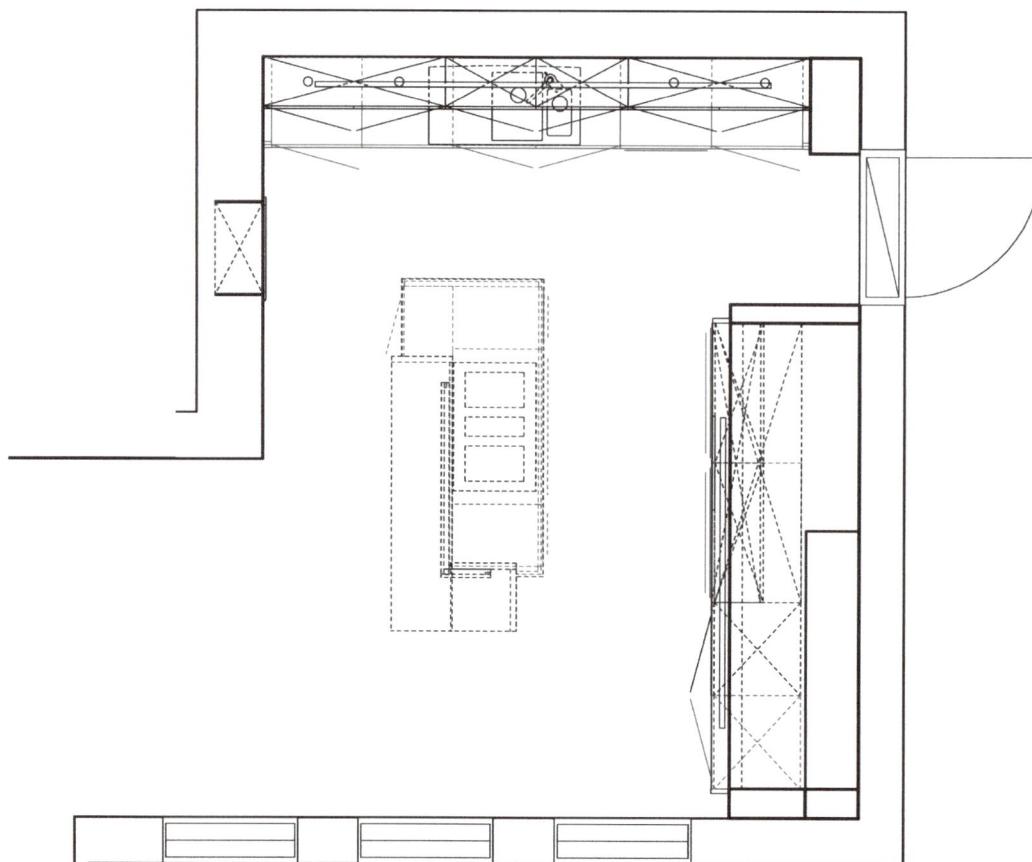

Orphic
Oxide Artstone

Natural
Carini Walnut
Cabinets

Abstract
Natural Carini
Walnut

Orphic
Kiruna Grigio
Artstone

Bronze Tint
Mirror

MODULAR DESIGN

Modular Design grew out of involvement in the building of exhibition stands incorporating two complete designer kitchens

As someone who has been involved in the Kitchen Industry for 40+ years, I've developed a wide experience of the different aspects as to what this entails. This encompasses both kitchen and product design, manufacture, installation and project management – to which you can add the experience of running a business. Modular Design has become a pet project of mine.

Modular Design grew out of involvement in the building of exhibition stands incorporating two complete designer kitchens. The issue relates to having only 10 to 20 hours to create such from scratch – and with no possibility of running over. We developed this to a fine art, and hence my fascination with incorporating lessons learnt to real life kitchens.

If it was possible to build an exhibition kitchen in under 10 hours, why wasn't this possible on live projects? Pre-planning and modularisation are the key. Everything prior to installation of the kitchen has to be completed: structural considerations, services, flooring, decorating, etc. Beyond this, every aspect of the kitchen furniture, work surfaces, appliances, sinks, taps, etc. must all be planned and pre-prepared in advance of arrival on site. This project is a great example of Modular Design.

The reality of a dry exhibition fit against a fully operational kitchen is vast – but lessons can be learnt. Pre-planning, modularisation and highly effective project management can all reduce the timescale and costs involved in kitchen installation. The skilled labour necessary for designer kitchens is expensive; reducing the timeframe saves money.

+ KITCHEN DISPLAY PRESENTED AT THE HOMEBUILDING & RENOVATING SHOW 2014

Carrying out a kitchen project in London is costly. The reasons for this include labour, travel, accommodation, living expenses, parking and many other aspects. So enacting Modular Design principles, as in this particular case for a project in Chiswick, made total sense. This was a kitchen for great mates who'd requested my design help and advice – an added complication being that they reside in Australia (this being their London pad when in the UK), hence all decisions had to be made remotely.

I had minor involvement in the design of the new extension, as this was to be a mirror image of their next door neighbours' property (who'd already embarked on their own project). One major change instigated by me related to incorporating pocket doors from the living/dining area and placing these centrally. This involved the removal of the wall between the hall and living/dining area, thus creating additional floor space, as the front door to the kitchen passageway was no longer required.

The kitchen was to be in the internal end of the new ground floor extension, and intended to incorporate a living/relaxing area to work in conjunction with a new contemporary patio/terrace via bi-fold doors. This was a perfect scenario for Modular Design – which in this case consisted of three stand-alone modules. These included a wet area, a centre island incorporating the hob and breakfast bar, plus a large tall bank containing ovens, fridge, freezer, cocktail cabinet and plenty of storage.

A further advantage of Modular Design is that work surfaces can be manufactured in advance from drawings, rather than templating these once the furniture is installed (which avoids delayed installation). The cost of templating saved money, as the kitchen was completed without requiring additional site visits. A major saving if operating from a distance, as was the case here.

Carrying out a kitchen project in London is costly.
The reasons for this include labour, travel, accommodation, living expenses, parking, & many other aspects.

This was a perfect scenario for Modular Design – which in this case consisted of three stand-alone modules

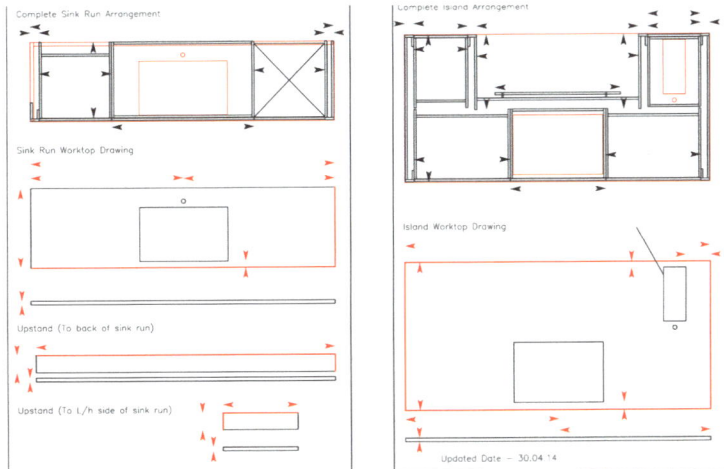

Complete Sink Run Arrangement

Sink Run Worktop Drawing

Upstand (To back of sink run)

Upstand (To L/h side of sink run)

Complete Island Arrangement

Island Worktop Drawing

Updated Date – 30.04.14

+ MODULAR WORKTOPS PRODUCED TO DRAWINGS PRIOR TO FIT

All structural & service elements were completed prior to the installation of the kitchen

The secret to Modular Design relates to a dry-fit. All structural and service elements were completed prior to the installation of the kitchen. This included the flooring: in this case, large oak planks from the front to the back of the house. All services being completed as far as possible in advance was critical. This included water, waste, electrics, extraction, heating, etc. An important element was a first coat of paint on the walls and ceiling, the main building contractor being responsible for such.

Incorporating Modular Design techniques (by necessity) tends to simplify the design. It's important to take on-board the significance of all the many products involved: furniture, appliances, sinks, taps, work surfaces, lighting, internal management systems and how they all combine together in relation to installation and project management. In this instance, the kitchen was completed and made operational by a team of two within three 8-hour days. I rest my case as to the benefits.

The before and after plans help to identify the structural changes. The photography of the finished article demonstrates the decision to mix finishes and materials: oak veneered stained furniture with high gloss elements, handleless and handles, stainless steel appliances, and quartz marble effect work surfaces. All combine together to create a highly functional kitchen, yet encompassing an understated but dramatic effect.

I've been lucky enough to be royally entertained here over many years, so I can vouch to the effectiveness of this kitchen.

EXISTING REAR ELEVATION   EXISTING SIDE ELEVATION   PROPOSED REAR ELEVATION   PROPOSED SIDE ELEVATIONS

EXISTING GROUND FLOOR PLAN   EXISTING FIRST FLOOR PLAN   PROPOSED GROUND FLOOR PLAN   PROPOSED FIRST FLOOR PLAN

+ EXISTING PROPERTY LAYOUT

+ PROPOSED LAYOUT

+ ROOM PREPARED PRIOR TO THE ARRIVAL OF THE KITCHEN

Modular Design
Alternative 1
Project 006

Inspiration

ANTIPODEAN ALTERNATIVE:
From the Other Side of the World to a More Classic Vibe

My great mates from Oz required a contemporary timeless kitchen – so here an alternative. Insights aims to highlight the wide variations that are possible within the same footprint. This a more classic design incorporating Shaker painted furniture with radiused features softening the over-all perspective. An apt demonstration of contrasting attributes in relation to performance and looks.

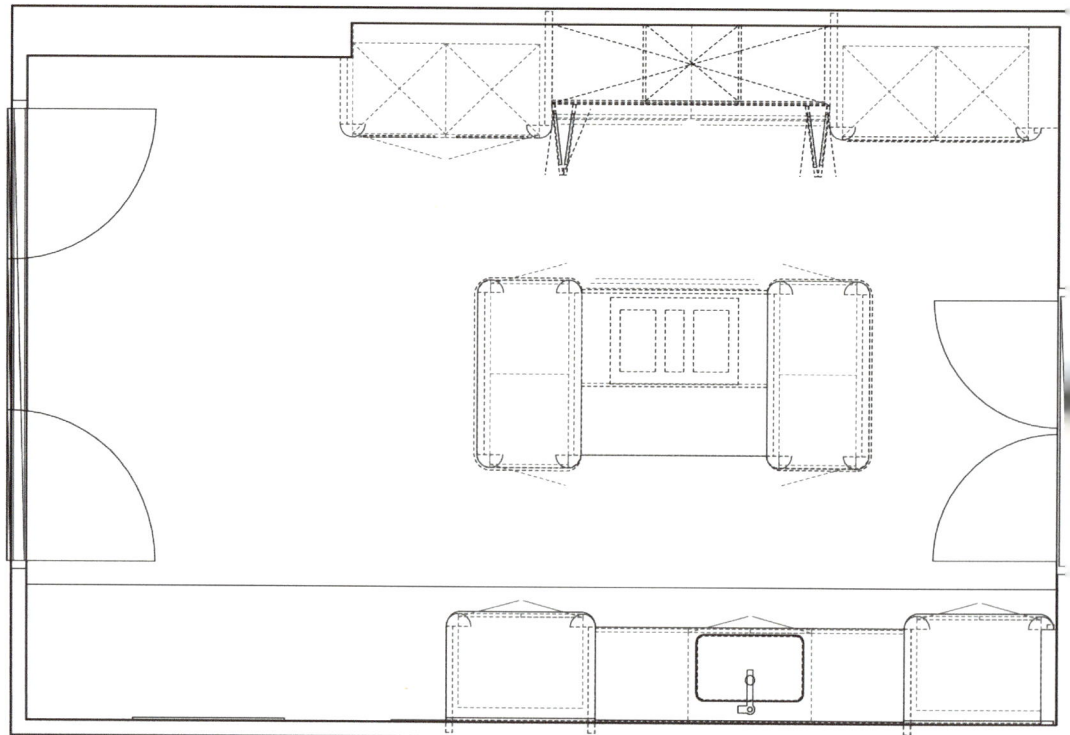

Cashmere Smooth Flat Painted

Pure Oak

Grey Tint Mirror

Kaisersberg Oak Cabinets

Midnight Grey Grained Painted

Natural Carini Walnut Cabinets

Pure Blue Grey Stained Oak

Fluted Glass

Modular Design
Alternative 2
Project 006

GOTHIC INSPIRATION:
A Change of Colour
Detail, Style, & Look

A bold dark colour interspersed with a variety of traditional aspects provides a totally different context to both the actual kitchen and the previous alternate proposal. A more imposing and latter-day feel is generated via the incorporation of classic features, chimney canopy and the striking three sided breakfast bar. Specifically for those who hark back to a more ancestral feel and sophistication.

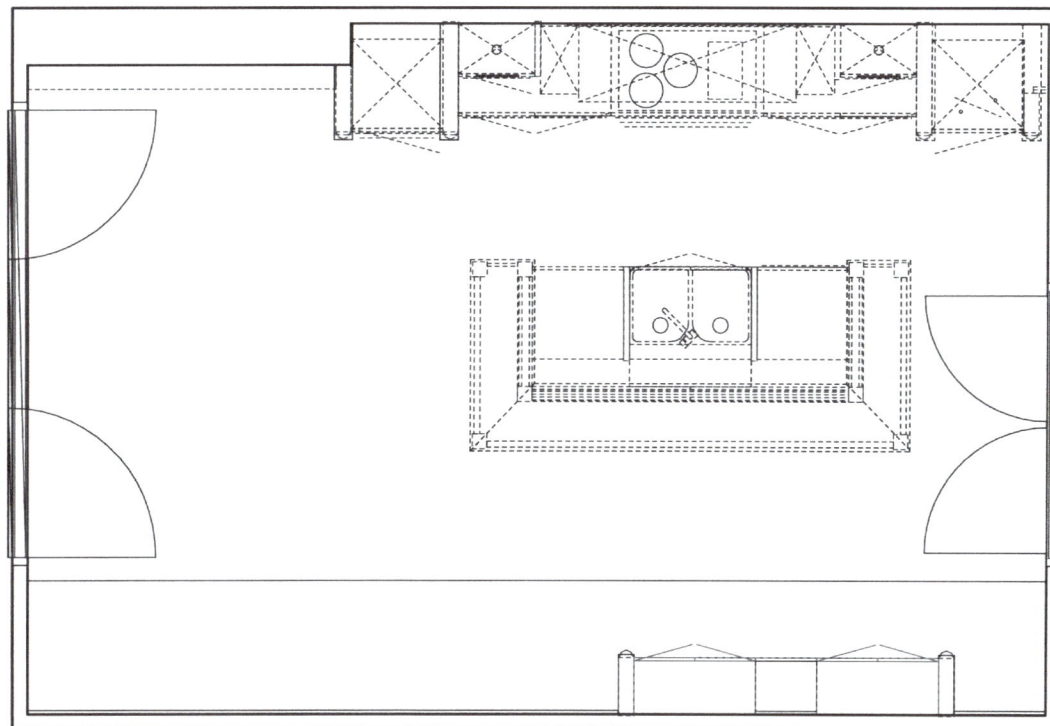

PASSIVHAUS PERFECTION

Callerton works in close conjunction with Potton at their Show Centre & Self Building Academy

The cost of living and energy crisis make this project highly pertinent. Callerton, as previous 'Insights' projects have alluded, work in close conjunction with Potton at their Show Centre and Self Building Academy, regarding the design and installation of kitchens for the various show-houses involved in this unique and highly innovative complex.

Potton's most recent project involved building a house to Passivhaus standard – which, in the interests of the planet, living in a warm and comfortable highly-efficient home with extremely low running costs, is something we should all pay greater attention to. The simple economics at a time of rampant energy costs makes for an interesting case-study.

We had no involvement in the design and layout of the new Passivhaus show home, this being provided by their architects HTA Design (specialists in this field) and Potton's own in-house team. Our brief related to creating a kitchen within a designated area, and this helped to demonstrate an exciting design-led kitchen can be achieved within a restricted budget.

+ POTTON SELF BUILD SHOW CENTRE

Our brief related to creating a kitchen within a designated area

It's essential not to pierce the external thermal membrane –
thought is required in relation to pipes, wiring, extraction, & more

Before moving onto the kitchen incorporated into the 'Elsworth' – Potton's contemporary Passivhaus – an observation. Rather than attempting to explain all that's involved in creating a Passivhaus, the benefits of such, and the build of this particular project – Google 'Potton Passivhaus' and visit their website for a series of insightful articles on the subject.

Designing and installing a kitchen for a Passivhaus involves taking on board a number of points. It's critical not to pierce the external thermal membrane – hence thought is required in relation to pipes, wiring, extraction, fixings, screws, etc. Traditionally, cooker hood extraction vented via an external wall – yet with heat retention and recovery crucial elements in relation to a Passivhaus – is not possible. Lessons need to be learned in relation to more conventional house projects.

As can be deduced from the plans, the project involved open-plan kitchen, living and dining – an aspect of Passivhaus design. The kitchen area is enclosed on three sides, and open on the fourth to the rest of the house, with a separate utility and rear entrance leading from this. A further element related to the long low-height window within the rear elevation.

With the 'Elsworth' very much a contemporary style of house, the decision was made; the kitchen should follow suit. Another aspect of the original design brief related to demonstrating that kitchen budgets don't have to be open-ended to ensure form, function and style are attainable. The kitchen for the Passivhaus show home is a great example of such.

+ PLAN OF GROUND FLOOR

Sleek Simple Lines

As a rule of thumb, the furniture element of a contemporary high tech kitchen requires less of the budget than more traditional designs – hence the reason for incorporating Monza handleless cabinetry from Callerton. Mixing two finishes with a contrasting ultra-thin glass effect work surface, with matching upstand taken up to the feature window, all add to the sleek simple lines. The raised plinth height and mirror finish below the centre island is a further subtle touch.

With the house design open-plan and based around a central courtyard theme, it was important the kitchen should be understated and blend with this. The large ceramic floor tiles and terrazzo effect central courtyard element influenced the choice of matt white furniture for the sink run and tall bank, with contrasting matt Fjord for the island and wall cabinets. The kitchen follows simple geometric lines, but nonetheless eminently stylish and functional.

The importance of the heat exchange unit and the recycling of waste heat within a Passivhaus led to the extraction and related pipework being built into a bulkhead above the island, adding an architectural element to the design. This was also ideal for the provision of effective lighting over the central preparation area. Positioning the hob within the island, looking out towards the main core of the house, enables those cooking to engage and interact with others.

The tall furniture bank houses an efficient single and combi oven, plus integrated fridge/freezer, all from Bosch. The choice of appliances within a Passivhaus is an important one – efficiency and low running costs are significant elements of Passivhaus standard. These Bosch appliances, plus the dishwasher, fitted the bill – hence their incorporation. The tall cabinet to the right of the ovens houses a Blum space tower providing highly effective and necessary storage.

This is an interesting and thought-provoking kitchen case-study in relation to energy efficiency, as well as designing to a restricted budget. The CAD drawings and imagery aptly demonstrate this particular project, but of further interest are the subsequent alternative designs which examine contrasting layouts, styles and functionality.

+ LOW-ENERGY & HIGH-QUALITY BUILDING

+ KITCHEN DESIGN AGREED PRIOR TO THE BUILD COMMENCING

This kitchen serves as a case-study in both energy efficiency & budget-restricted design

Pure
Oak

Pure White
Smooth
Flat Painted

Kaisersberg
Oak
Cabinets

Passivhaus Perfection
Alternative 1
Project 007

Inspiration

ARCHITECTURAL ELEMENTS:
The Orientation of Windows & Doors

Creating a new build house or construction of an extension provides the opportunity to position windows and doors to suit. But worth bearing in mind the reconfiguring of such within an existing building can transform the form and function of your kitchen. The Passivhaus layout dramatically changes in this instance via incorporation of three windows rather the long, low single version.

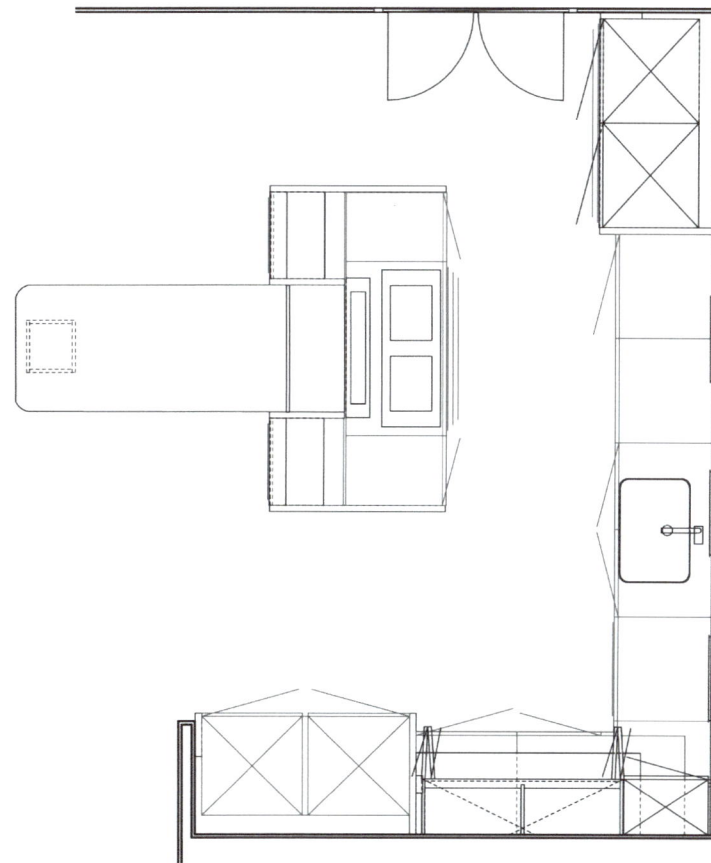

Passivhaus Perfection
Alternative 2
Project 007

Inspiration

LAID BACK & EASY GOING:
Kitchen Creation to Amplify an Individuals Characteristics

This alternative design possesses a free and easy Scandinavian feel - if that suits your character, your design specialist is in a position to exploit and weave such into the project. The combination of timber and pastels within the same piece of furniture produces an interesting effect. The tall to ceiling element combined with low level contrasting cabinetry above the window - is highly effective.

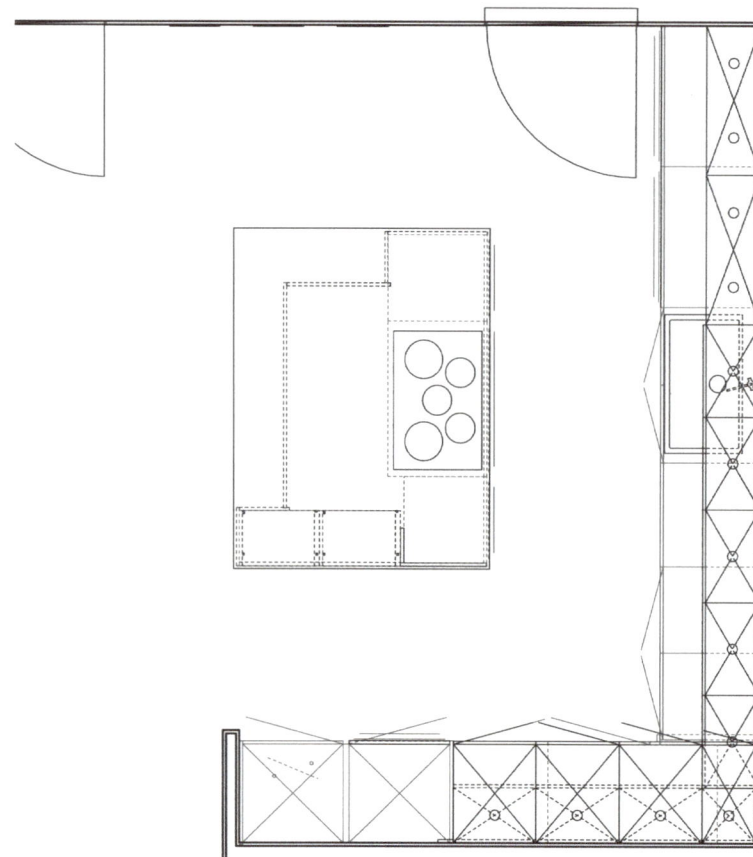

Monza
Matt
Reed Green

Onyx
Grey
Cabinets

Abstract
Expressions
Tobacco
Halifax Oak

Orphic
Scuro
Oak Chalet

Abstract
Onyx
Grey

ABOUT TURN

The doctors and their two teenage children had thought long & hard about redeveloping the ground floor of their property

Many years ago, a great family friend asked if I could assist his daughter and son-in-law (both young doctors) with designing a kitchen for their city centre flat in Edinburgh. Fast forward twenty or so years and I was approached once again for advice with reference to a re-design of the kitchen in their now-family home – an impressive town house.

The doctors and their two teenage children had thought long and hard about redeveloping the ground floor of their property, and had planning permission in place for a new garden-room extension. The issue being that this left little scope and opportunity to reconfigure the kitchen layout, as they wished to retain the existing fireplace and seating area.

As ever, establishing my clients' design criteria was the first step in the journey. In this particular case, they'd spent much time and effort researching and discussing their various wishes, aims and ambitions for their new kitchen. As a designer, this is most welcome and aids the design process. Their list contained the following:

As ever, establishing my clients' design criteria was the first step in the journey

The new kitchen was to be family and entertaining oriented – they were adventurous chefs. A table and chairs for formal dining, and a breakfast bar for more casual fare. A further stipulation related to incorporating Callerton's Deco radius end features (a design detail from their first Callerton kitchen). The appliance requirements were pre-set and involved the following: a Siemens oven, combi oven, large induction hob, tall larder fridge with freezer compartment, integrated dishwasher and effective built-in extraction. A Franke 2½ bowl stainless steel sink and tap was also specified.

+ KITCHEN & LIVING AREA PRIOR TO REDEVELOPMENT

The new garden room extension provided little scope to develop & expand the kitchen

+ INITIAL DESIRE TO ADD A GARDEN ROOM

Clients such as these, who do their homework in advance, help to ensure the products incorporated fit their specific needs and requirements. My trusty 'Design Criteria' document in this instance was redundant, as many decisions were already concluded. Clients spending time in advance, establishing their requirements, is a major benefit to designers.

An area that did a full 'About Turn' related to the initial thoughts in relation to style. The existing kitchen incorporated bespoke traditional timber furniture, and something along these lines had been their original thinking. They eventually did a complete volte face - but I'm getting ahead of myself, as a further aspect turned the original concept upside down.

As discussed earlier, the new garden room extension provided little scope to develop and expand the kitchen – particularly in light of the fireplace and seating area having to be retained. Having carried out my initial site survey and established my clients' thoughts in relation to their design criteria, I took this away and transferred these to my trusty drawing board – which confirmed my suspicion that radically redeveloping the kitchen would prove an issue.

What ensued was a discussion and a question which proved pivotal in redefining the whole project: "Have you considered removing the wall between the current kitchen and dining room"? Having established that the answer was "No," I suggested creating a set of 3D CAD drawings to demonstrate how this would radically alter things. Prior to doing so, I invited the family to visit a Callerton showroom to demonstrate a further possible extreme option.

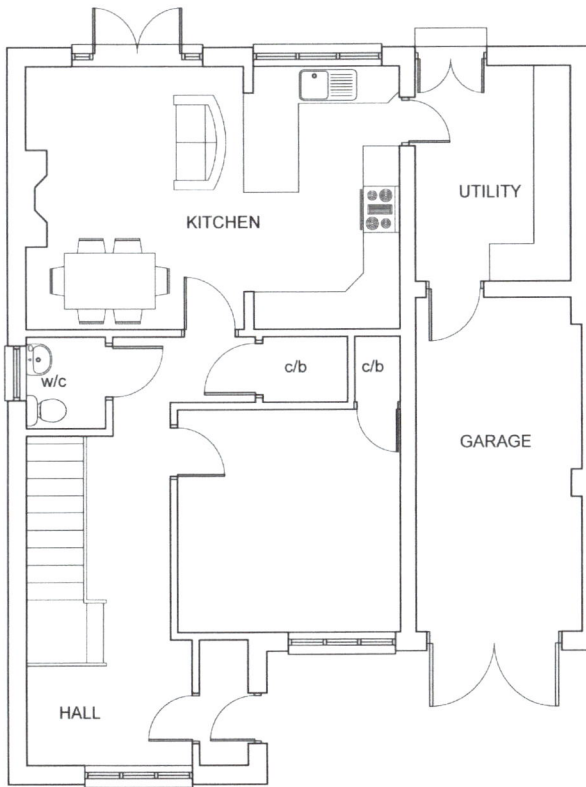

+ EXISTING PROPERTY LAYOUT

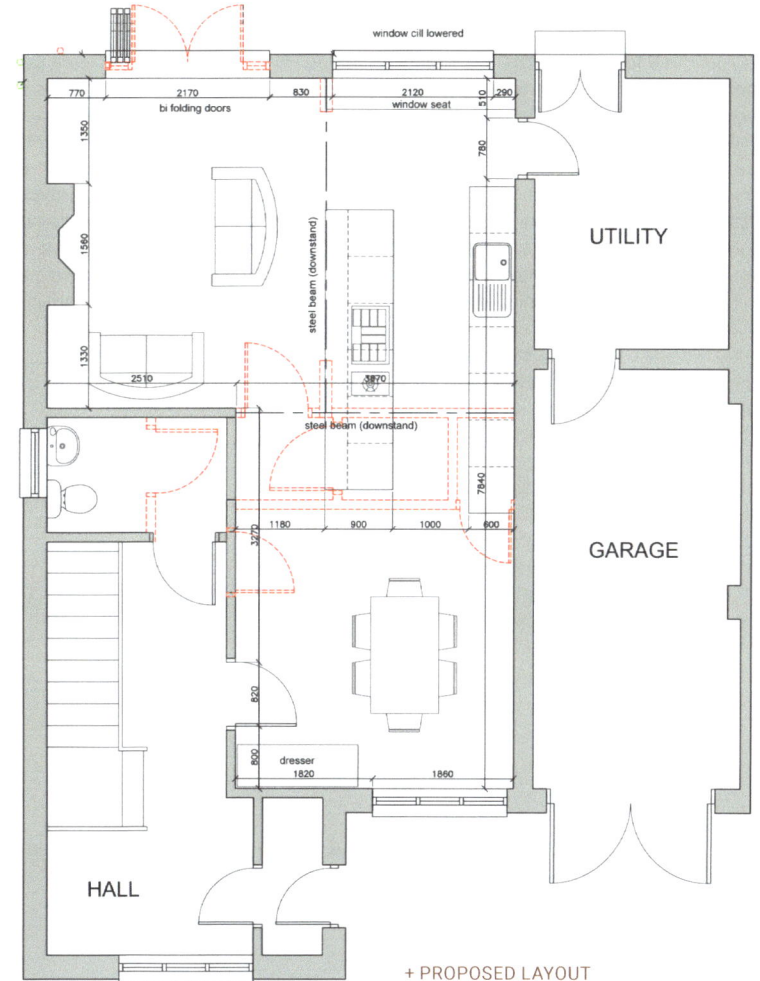

+ PROPOSED LAYOUT

"Have you considered removing the wall between the current kitchen & dining room"?

As a designer, my role is to demonstrate what is possible & open my clients' eyes to alternatives

My aim was to demonstrate the possibility of a radical change in style from a classic Shaker look to the possibility of a crossover/hybrid design incorporating both traditional and contemporary elements. The fascinating thing was that they took this concept on-board immediately and pushed the boundaries even further towards a modern idiom.

As a designer, my role is to demonstrate what is possible and open my clients' eyes to alternatives. It's extremely satisfying when people engage with this (as per this particular instance), and the project henceforth heads in a totally different direction. From here I produced two sets of CAD drawings demonstrating that the orientation of the kitchen could be reversed. We'll concentrate on the final design for now, the alternative design being highlighted in the CAD concepts.

The CAD imagery and finishes were almost identical to the actual final article. It's always gratifying when clients embrace more radical colours in advance: Callerton's Matt Monza handleless in Fjord (blue), contrasted with Mocca stained flat veneered oak doors – set off with Deco radius features and glazed cabinetry. The shark-nosed work surfaces were a further piece de la resistance, also chosen in advance during the earlier showroom consultation.

I leave you with images of the finished article, which aptly demonstrate the wisdom of my clients' 'About Turn'.

+ DESIGN AGREED & ROOM PREPARED PRIOR TO THE KITCHENS ARRIVAL ON SITE

Cathcart
Smooth
Flat Painted

Kaisersberg
Oak
Cabinets

Sail
Smooth
Flat Painted

Pure
Oak

Grey Tint
Mirror

About Turn
Alternative 1
Project 008

Inspiration

ADDITIONS TO TRADITION:
Contemporary Handless Combines with Classic

At first sight this would appear to be a traditional/ classic style of kitchen – but look closer and notice the incorporation of contemporary handless furniture elements. The mixing of genres can make for something different and individual. Note the change in layout from the existing - with the wet area moving to the far end of the room. A project such as this provides for a variety of diverse options.

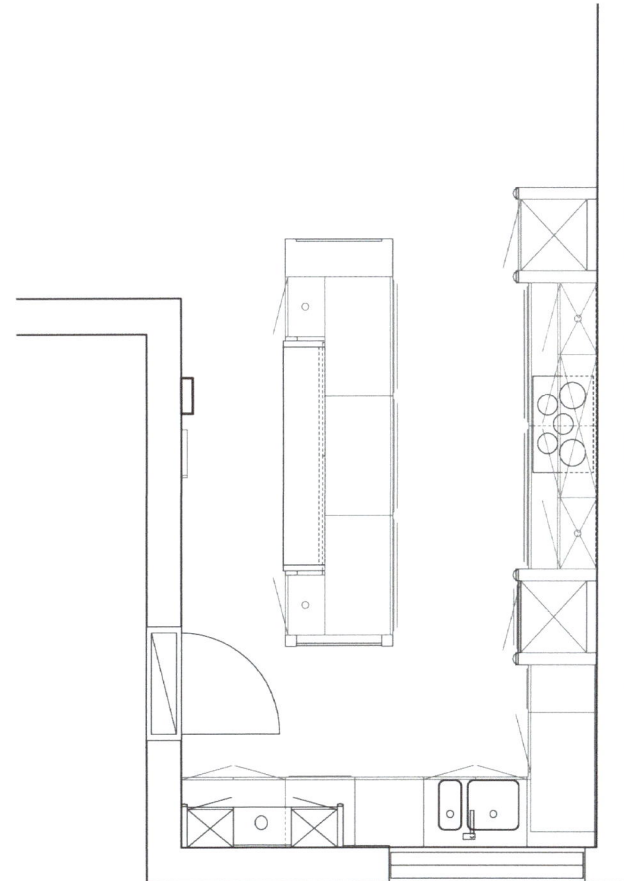

About Turn
Alternative 2
Project 008

Inspiration

HIDDEN FROM VIEW:
Presenting a Streamlined Demeanour

The orientation of the kitchen transferred to one end – maximises living space. A sleek minimalist design with storage and functionality in the main hidden from view. Includes a contemporary version of a butler's pantry providing practicality and an out of sight home for the coffee machine, kettle, toaster and other associated paraphernalia. The 3 designs highlight the disparate nature of kitchens.

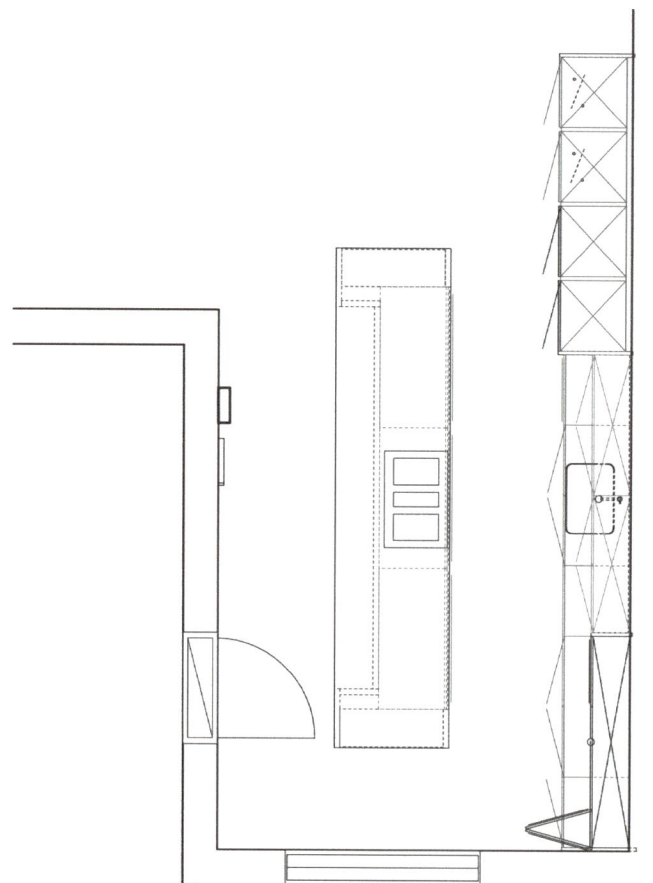

Abstract
Kaisersberg
Oak

Kaisersberg
Oak
Cabinets

Monza
Matt
Black

Abstract
Onyx
Grey

MAGNIFICENT MILCHESTER

Potton's unique Show Village and Self Build Academy initiative requires no further explanation, as we've previously featured two such kitchen projects in earlier 'Insights' articles. Magnificent Milchester is an apt title, for the house lives up to such an accolade. The property is a modern day take on an Edwardian Rectory, and a truly outstanding residence.

+ ORIGINAL KITCHEN & FAMILY ROOM

The property is a modern day take on an Edwardian Rectory, a truly outstanding residence

Callerton's partnership with Potton led to our involvement in the update and reconfiguration of the Milchester's kitchen. The project involved a major transformation of the original house design and layout (built some 30+ years ago). It is a great example of how tastes, necessities and requirements have developed over the intervening years.

The images and plans of the original dated property demonstrate how Potton's decision to not only refurbish the internal layout but also upgrade the exterior has paid dividends. How we utilise our homes in today's world is different to the past – more bathrooms, open-plan kitchen, living and dining... all highlight some of the must-have elements.

The imagery of the original kitchen demonstrates not only how dated and uninspiring this was, but also how inefficient and lacking in character it seemed for such an imposing house. The same was true of the family room and conservatory beyond. Hence Potton's decision to turn three into one – forming one large kitchen, living, and breakfast area.

A major transformation of the original house design— highlighting how tastes & requirements evolve over decades

The Milchester is a great example as to the orientation of a house and access to light and a view. Turning the old kitchen, conservatory and family room into one, with the addition of large bi-fold doors plus long low-level windows in two of the other elevations, transforms the space. It's now light and airy; throw open the bi-fold doors and the garden and patio are incorporated into the room. It's worth taking such considerations on-board when designing your dream kitchen.

The design criteria instruction and information focused on a simple Shaker style – the aim being that the kitchen, living and breakfast elements should meld together in harmony. The incorporation of a chimney breast worked not only from an aesthetic point of view, but also in hiding an unsightly RSJ required to support the floor above. Structural alterations can often be hidden/disguised by incorporation of such within elements of the kitchen furniture.

+ KITCHEN, CONSERVATORY & FAMILY ROOM CONVERTED TO ONE SPACE

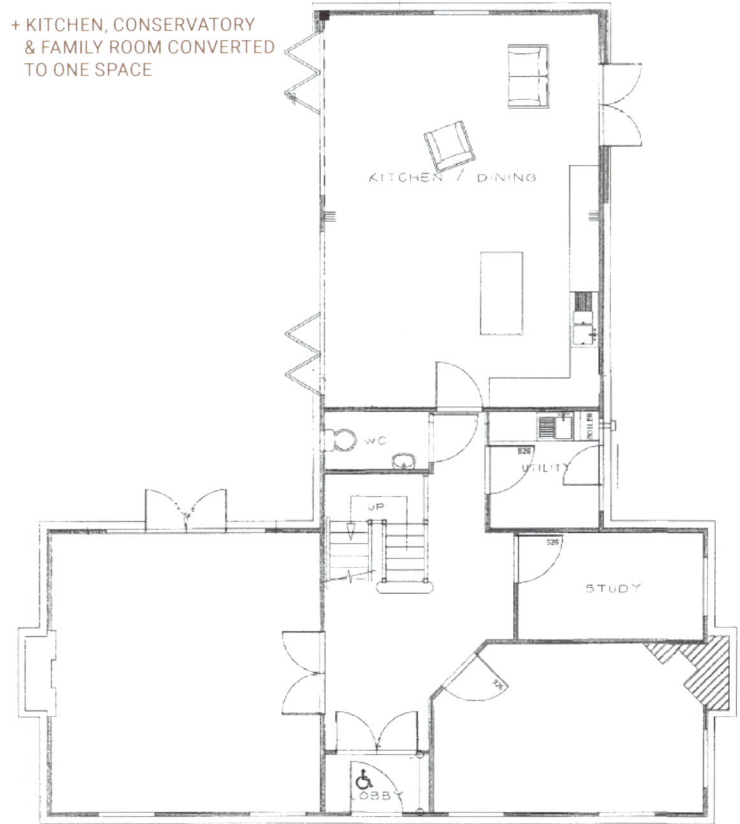

+ EXISTING PROPERTY LAYOUT

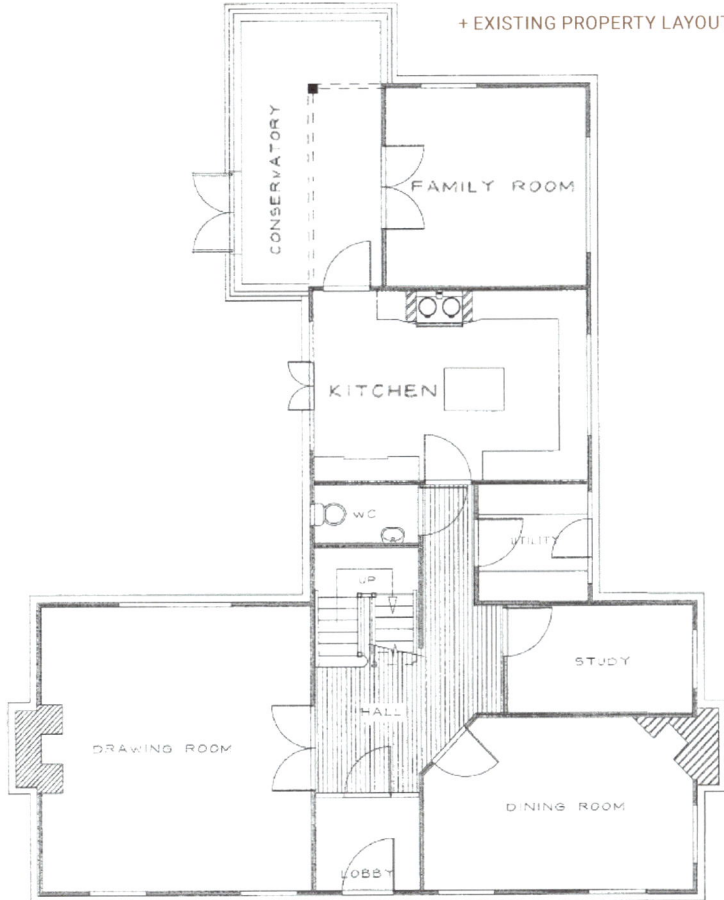

Large bi-fold doors and low-level windows usher in a new era of light & airiness to the Milchester

A Belfast sink & imposing tap take centre stage on a kitchen island designed for both form and function

The ubiquitous Belfast sink was specified with an imposing tap, to be incorporated into a centre island. The chimney breast brought about the decision for two Neff stainless steel under-ovens and a long narrow induction hob to be installed. To echo this, and with a further nod to the contemporary, a tall stainless steel fridge/freezer was specified. Two further elements dictating the layout related to a table to seat eight, and the living area to incorporate a settee and two easy chairs.

The island was constrained by the dining and living areas; this incorporated a double Belfast sink with an integrated dishwasher to one side and a pull-out recycling waste bin to the other, all supported by four hefty legs which provided a sense of solidity. The island's Dekton work-surface matches the backsplash to the rear of the chimney breast.

Balance and symmetry is achieved on the back wall, with glazed wall cabinets central to either side of the chimney breast. The contrasting dark grey break-fronted work surface makes a further statement. Unusually, it would appear there are no pan-drawers. In fact, large internal pan-drawers are hidden behind the doored cabinetry. A simple detail, but often missed, is the addition of the ceiling cornice which ensures that the chimney breast appears structural.

The final furniture element relates to the rear internal wall incorporating an open/glazed dresser to one side, and the imposing stainless steel fridge/freezer flanked by two extremely useful tall cabinets incorporating internal Blum space towers. The long-term benefit of effective internal management systems should never be underestimated.

I leave you with the CAD imagery and photography of the finished article as to whether we fulfilled our brief.

Balance & Symmetry

Accuracy in planning & execution underscores the value of collaboration with a knowledgeable & timely team

Before concluding, I would like to make this point: working in conjunction with professionals from the Potton Team made this particular project extremely easy from Callerton's perspective. Being presented in advance with accurate working drawings that truly relate to the finished article, as well as all the structural and service work carried out meticulously and on time, emphasises the importance of working with a Team who know their trade.

If you're ever passing St Neots, I highly recommend a visit to Potton's Show Village – it'll be well worthwhile.

Magnificent Milchester
Alternative 1
Project 009

Inspiration

ANGLED & ANGULAR:
Plain & Spartan Creates
a Powerful Effect

The diversity of design options within the world of kitchens is immense: - From classic to contemporary and a myriad of options in-between. This an example of catering for minimalist requirements - but none the less impressive. The exposed brickwork, novel take on a chimney canopy, impressive use of worksurfaces, fresh approach to open shelving – make a bold statement.

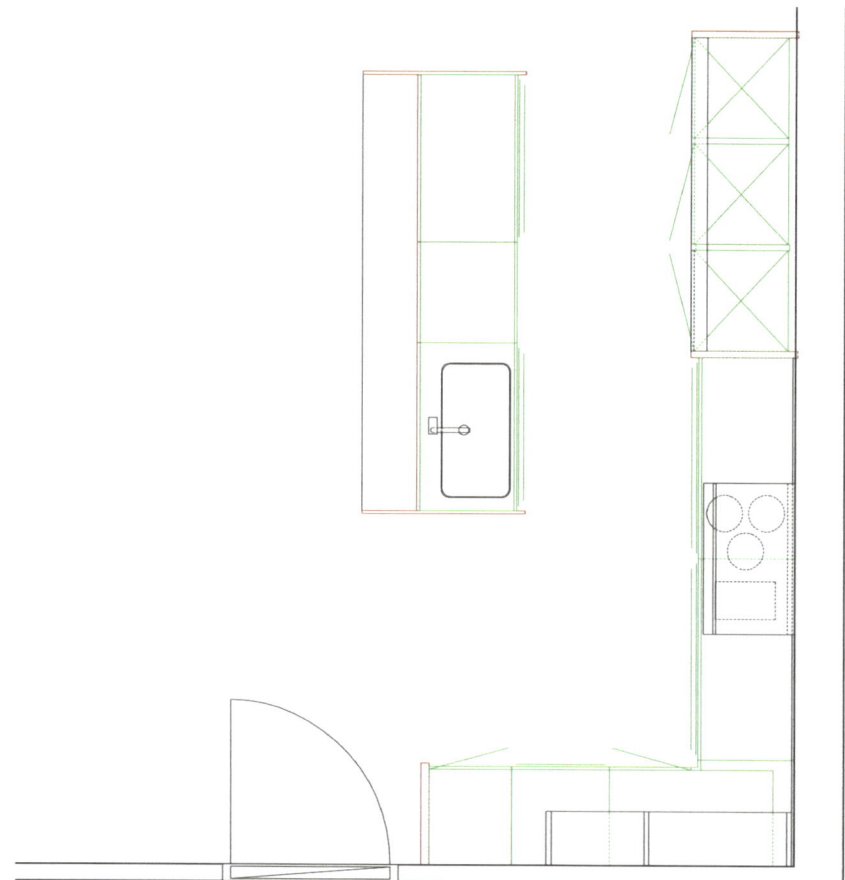

Abstract Expressions
Black Gold
Metal Slate

Onyx
Grey
Cabinets

Monza
Matt Frost
White

Pure
Mocca
Stained Oak

Copper Effect
Profile

Dark Sky
Smooth
Flat Painted

Natural Hamilton Oak Cabinets

Lark White
Smooth
Flat Painted

Abstract Expressions Pewter Halifax Oak

Magnificent Milchester
Alternative 2
Project 009

Inspiration

COLOURFUL CHARACTERISTICS:
Distinctive Open & Doored Cabinetry Combination

Doored and glazed cabinetry combined with a distinct and varied array of open-shelving generates an interesting and dramatic outcome. Add in contrasting colours for a further dimension. In such circumstances lighting is a critical element to maximising the ambiance. Other aspects of note relate to the work-surface detail and architectural ceiling feature incorporating extraction and illumination.

BEAUTIFUL BARN

Potton's stylish take on a customary timber barn leaves you with a multitude of options, as to defining the internal layout to suit your lifestyle and modus operandi

Many aspire to that quintessential rural barn conversion. The problem arises as to availability of such in your desired locality, the complexity and cost of such projects, as well as an inability to define the timescale. There's an excellent alternative, however, which is ably demonstrated by Callerton's involvement with Potton at their Show Centre and Self Build Academy.

Potton's impressive Whickhambrook show home, on display at St Neots, is a modern day take on a traditional wooden barn. If you can acquire a suitable site, this may well prove to be the more realistic alternative. It offers the look, feel and style of a rural barn without all of the complexities, issues and drawbacks associated with involvement in the real thing.

The conversion of a traditional farm building into a home can be fraught with unforeseen issues, problems and cost overruns. Starting with a blank sheet of paper and developing your barn from scratch – with the incorporation of all the latest technology and ongoing economies associated with such – is made possible via the Whickhambrook.

Potton's stylish take on a customary timber barn leaves you with a multitude of options, as to defining the internal layout to suit your lifestyle and modus operandi. This is the beauty of working with a specialist house manufacturer who can not only alter the building to suit the orientation for your particular site, but also the layout and scale.

In this instance, Callerton were not involved at the time the house was originally built, but later in relation to updating the kitchen. This brought about an interesting conundrum in that the whole ground floor was tiled throughout and the stipulation was that we were not to disturb these in any way. Hence the water, waste, wiring and services in the main had to remain in situ – which set parameters in relation to our re-design.

Callerton's Design Team were given a free hand, other than the fact that the style & look was to be more towards the contemporary – but with a nod to the kitchen being in a timber barn

Callerton's Design Team were given a free hand, other than the fact that the style and look was to be more towards the contemporary – but with a nod to the kitchen being in a timber barn. Hence the decision to combine handless high gloss furniture with a contemporary washed effect timber finish. This was subtly echoed within the Retro features which combine both high gloss and timber. The seamless Corian tops with integrated upstand add to the sleek appearance.

An added complication was introduced via the fact that the kitchen was to be utilised by Siemens for high-end cookery demonstrations and training purposes. Hence the layout of the single oven, combi oven, warming drawers and coffee machine on the back wall, and the hob and down-draught extraction located in the centre island. Down-draught extraction was essential, as the high pitched ceiling left little alternative. The rear wall also incorporates a large fridge and freezer.

The decision was to create three specific modules:
the tall appliance bank, the hob & preparation area within the centre island & the wet area

The decision was to create three specific modules: the tall appliance bank, the hob and preparation area within the centre island, and the wet area largely dictated by the inability to disturb the tiled floor. All of this was extremely practical and workable. The subtle touches of break-fronting to each of the three areas adds an extra dimension to the design.

The height of the back wall and the steep comb provided the opportunity to utilise extra tall furniture, which works well in relation to the balance and symmetry of the room. The subtle central cornice detail adds an extra touch. The large high gloss pan drawers below the ovens, lift-up cabinetry above and tall cupboards to either side all provide for excellent and accessible storage facilities, and this was added to via the extra height timber-effect cabinetry.

The central island provides further excellent storage via large pan-drawers to either side of the hob – sensible and practical. The rear of the island incorporates a breakfast bar with subtle lighting built into the high-gloss raised panel below. The ultra-thin Corian work-surface ensures no visible joints and adds to the overall sleek look.

The wet area incorporates a high gloss break-fronted element incorporating a double stainless steel under-mount Franke sink with a boiling water/filter tap, with a dishwasher to one side and recycling waste bin the other. This contrasted with set-back washed timber effect pan drawers to either side. Balance and symmetry were very much to the fore.

This was an excellent example of updating and replacing an existing kitchen and having to work within various pre-set guidelines and parameters. A fairly minimalist design, but in keeping with – and maintaining the ethos of – the wooden barn.

Our alternative CAD designs for the Whickhambrook explore the opportunity to further develop the potential this fascinating house design offers. Maintaining the footprint, but looking through the eyes of a client building off-plan rather than being constrained by this particular kitchen being a replacement, provides much food for thought.

Once again, I must reiterate that if you're looking for inspiration in relation to a new-build or a kitchen – please pay Potton a visit.

Beautiful Barn
Alternative 1
Project 010

Inspiration

FRESH PERSPECTIVE:
A New Build Offers
Up Opportunities

If building a Potton barn from scratch the opportunity to adapt the footprint or layout is substantial. This example retains the same footprint, but patio doors replace the existing sink window – providing the option to reconfigure the kitchen. The wet area now located below the windows in the gable end. An interesting Shaker hybrid design with a multitude of signature and feature items.

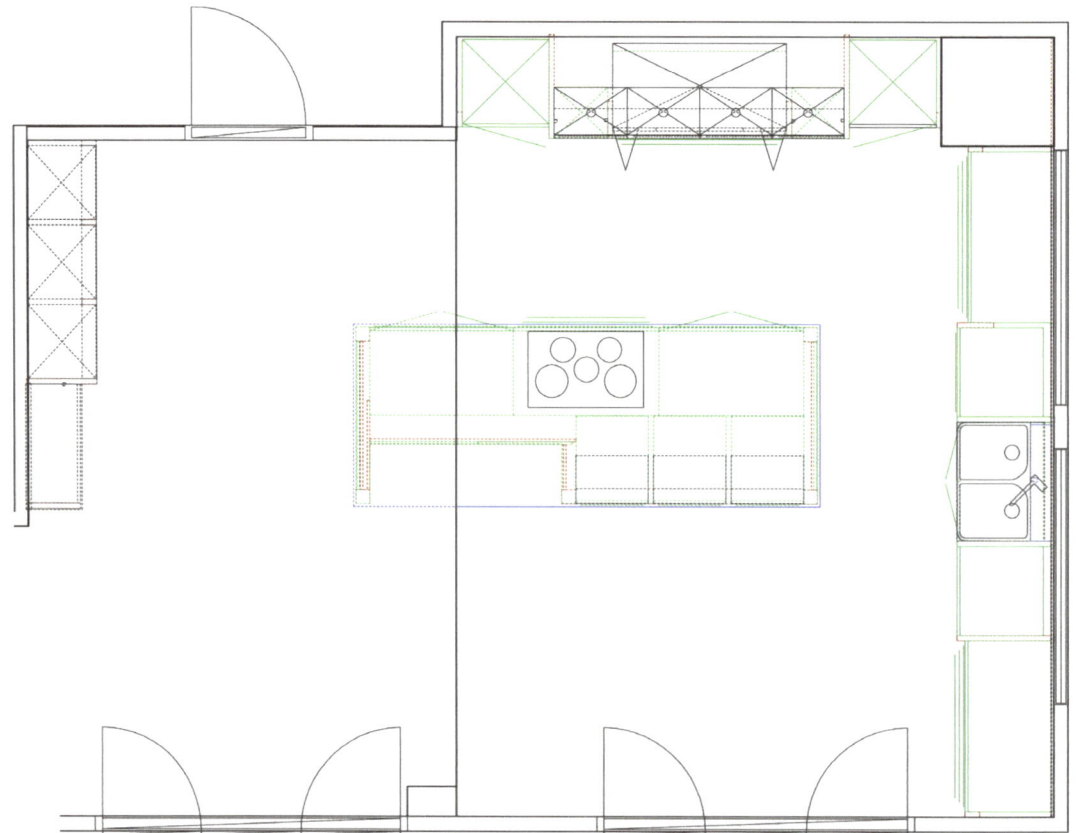

Galaxy Blue Smooth Flat Painted

Natural Carini Walnut Cabinets

North Grey Smooth Flat Painted

Pure Oak

Fluted Glass

Park Green
Smooth
Flat Painted

Kaisersberg
Oak
Cabinets

Pure
Dark Grey
Stained Oak

Brass Effect
Profile

Beautiful Barn
Alternative 2
Project 010

SIMPLE BUT STYLISH:
Restraint in Design
can Equate to
Spectacular Results

We're all different and view the World of design
and style in many different ways – hence the
importance of developing each project around
the needs and requirements of the individual.
This an excellent example of an element of
restraint producing a dramatic result. Balance
and symmetry, as well as the inclusion of
discrete but opposing materials, colours,
plus other aspects – work wonders.

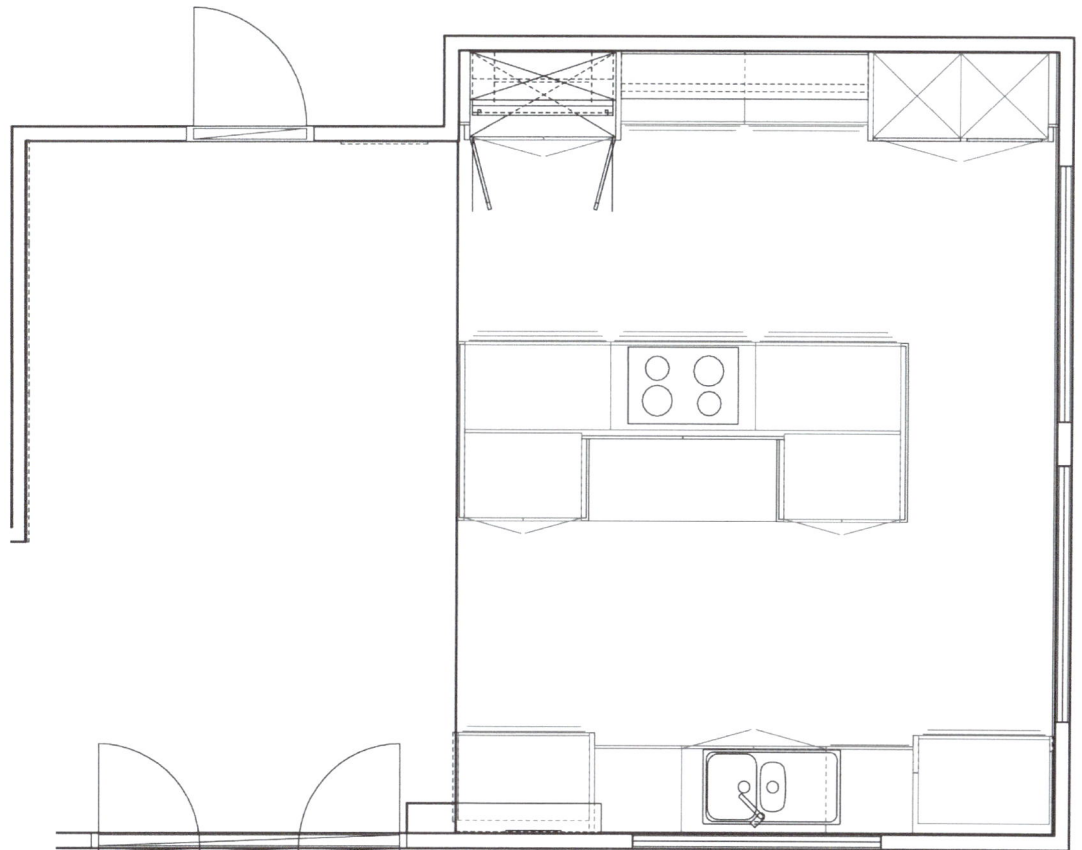

KITCHEN
DESIGN
SPECI

ALISTS

Explore the Artistry
of Kitchen Specialists,
Showcasing Timeless Creations
& Innovative Reimagination

Venturing beyond my designs, we explore the artistry of kitchen specialists, showcasing timeless creations and innovative reimagination.

Having had design input with the first ten of the twenty kitchen projects, I decided it would be an interesting exercise to look at those created by other designers and examine their approach to the task. Each case-study involves a Callerton kitchen (manufactured by us) but the design individual to one of our colleagues from our National Network of Design-led Kitchen Specialist Retailers.

Each kitchen tells a unique story, crafted by specialists from our National Network

Creating a successful design inspired kitchen is highly individual to the client and the working relationship established with their designer. Examining the methodology and working practises of 10 fellow designers and 10 contrasting projects aims to demonstrate the importance of this element.

Great design is timeless; our diverse kitchens are a testament to evolving creativity over 15 years

I raided Callerton's digital picture library as I wanted to demonstrate great design is timeless – with the assortment of projects going back in excess of 15 years. I've not detailed their individual age and leave you to judge their time-line. Each is a case-study in how the individual designer has gone about creating an inspiring and innovative kitchen that fulfils the needs and requirements of their client.

As per the first section we then re-examine and re-design each kitchen project, utilising the same footprint, but creating 2 alternative and contrasting designs. Design continually evolves and develops which is an exciting element of the design-led kitchen specialist world. I hope our efforts (this has had much input from colleagues) provide an indication of how diverse kitchens can be.

011
Extreme Restoration

012
Island Ingenuity

013
Design Divergence

014
Poignant Project

015

Pièce de Rèsistance

016
Grand Design

017
Minimalist Marvel

018
Salutary Style

019
Party Central

020
Perfect Situation

Peter – a long-time Callerton colleague and talented kitchen design specialist – hails from the North East of England, and he answered my initial question with zero hesitation. What category do you place this particular project: new build, extension, renovation, replacement or other? "Extreme Restoration" was his answer – hence the title.

Extreme
Restoration

Extreme Restoration
2016

The National Coal Board left the building on its last legs & unfit for human habitation

Peter explained that his clients took on the project after the National Coal Board left the building on its last legs and unfit for human habitation. This was a brave and inspiring move. They could see the potential, and were determined to restore and develop this into their dream home. Peter's clients deserve high praise for their foresight and tenacity, in that they and others like them ensure that the glorious heritage of buildings such as these are preserved for future generations.

Peter's clients deserve high praise for their foresight & tenacity

Peter was engaged & involved at an early stage in the project

The dramatic imagery taken during the restoration process aptly demonstrates the scale of the task in hand. Peter was full of praise for the vision and foresight of his clients, explaining that he was engaged and involved at an early stage in the project. His clients well understood the importance of ensuring their aims and ambitions for their new combined kitchen, living and dining area must fit together with the restoration, as well as the build schedule.

I wanted to understand Peter's modus operandi when engaging with clients, and how he extracted all the necessary information from them in order to be in a position to develop a design. His response being: "I tend to talk through wish lists, as I want to inspire them with both the design and functionality." He explained his opening line tends to relate to "Let's start with what we've dreamed about, and how that can work within the constraints of the building."

Let's start with what we've dreamed about

A further question I put to Peter: "In relation to the design, architecture and layout of the property, did you influence or impact this?" His reply was: "A little; the building is a historic property, and I had little scope regards the physical space. I had an influence in relation to windows and bi-fold doors to help maximise light within the room, as well as ensuring the kitchen and dining space melded with the garden and patio area."
The final imagery aptly demonstrates the result.

An aspect that intrigued me related to whether any particular architectural features in relation to the building had influenced Peter. "Because of the age of the property, features such as the necessity for a central ceiling beam and the low windows drove the layout of the room to a degree. But the standout feature, and one that adds dramatic effect, relates to exposing the combed ceiling and installing Velux roof-lights in the working area of the kitchen."

One of the hardest parts of a project such as this is a client's ability to visualise the space, especially when opening up a series of rooms. The CAD imagery highlights the importance of this.

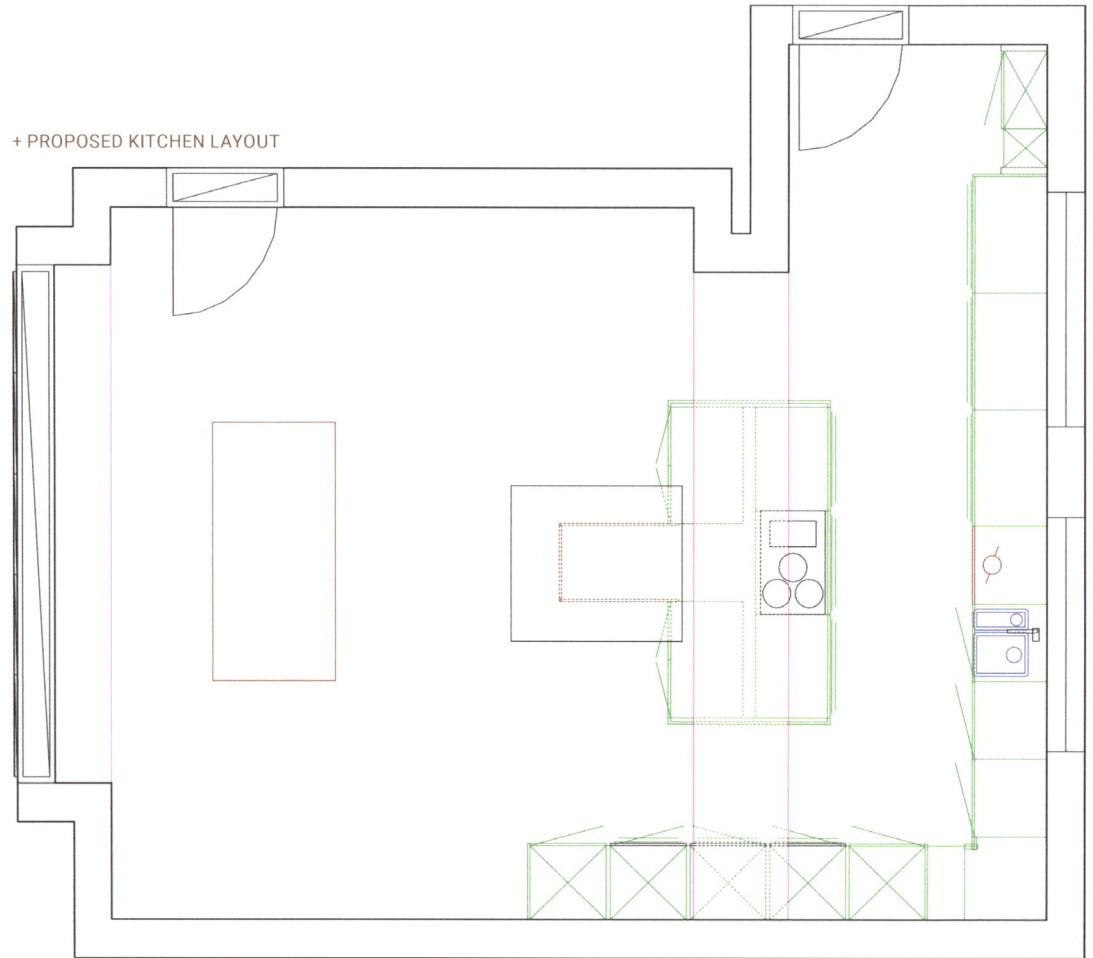

+ PROPOSED KITCHEN LAYOUT

Peter emphasised the importance of establishing his client's requirements and methodology when operating their new kitchen. An early aspect he likes to ratify relates to the appliances. In this case Neff, the client's preferred brand, and the line-up involved: Halogen hob, two ovens, combi oven/microwave, warming drawer, fridge/freezer, dishwasher and wine cabinet. The sink and tap configuration is a further factor Peter likes to establish early on.

A further question I asked of Peter was: "Did you influence your client's choices in relation to style and colour"? He explained as follows: "The primary colour was pretty much fixed prior to my involvement, but I was able to guide with the secondary colour as well as utilising a natural quartzite work surface on the island." The finished result was highly effective.

I was interested to hear about the importance Peter places on CAD (computer aided design) imagery to impart his vision of a kitchen design. "It's vital. One of the hardest parts of a project such as this is a client's ability to visualise the space, especially when opening up a series of rooms." The CAD imagery highlights the importance of this.

To truly comprehend the scale of the transformation involves comparing photography of the house during the early stages of the restoration and the finished result. I believe this to be a masterclass in how one should go about handling a kitchen in a renovation project. The relationship and understanding between client and their kitchen design specialist is absolutely crucial to ensuring that the final result truly fulfils all of their aims and ambitions.

A final question of Peter demonstrates that the above was achieved: "What aspect of the project gave you the most satisfaction?" The answer was: "Being involved from an early stage enabled me to see the project develop from start to finish – but the real standout moment was experiencing my client's reaction and their pride in their amazing new home."

The finished result was highly effective

Extreme Restoration
Alternative 1
Project 011

REDEFINING ELEGANCE:
A Fusion of Contrasting Hues & Innovative Design in Modern Kitchen Craftsmanship

From angular high tech contemporary to something completely different. The incorporation of painted furniture in contrasting colours, plus the addition of flat contemporary doors, a spectacular island with built in table, novel open shelving – add curved elements to the mix generates style and looks to turn heads. The functionality and practicality of the layout deserves mention.

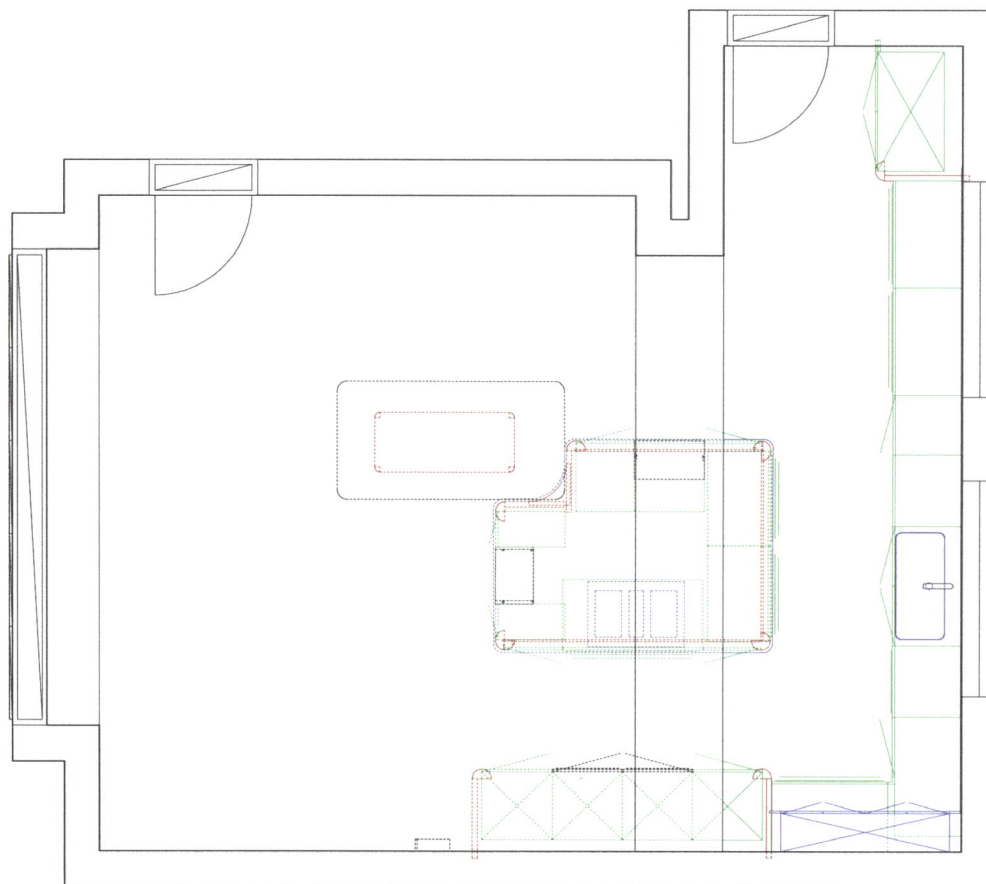

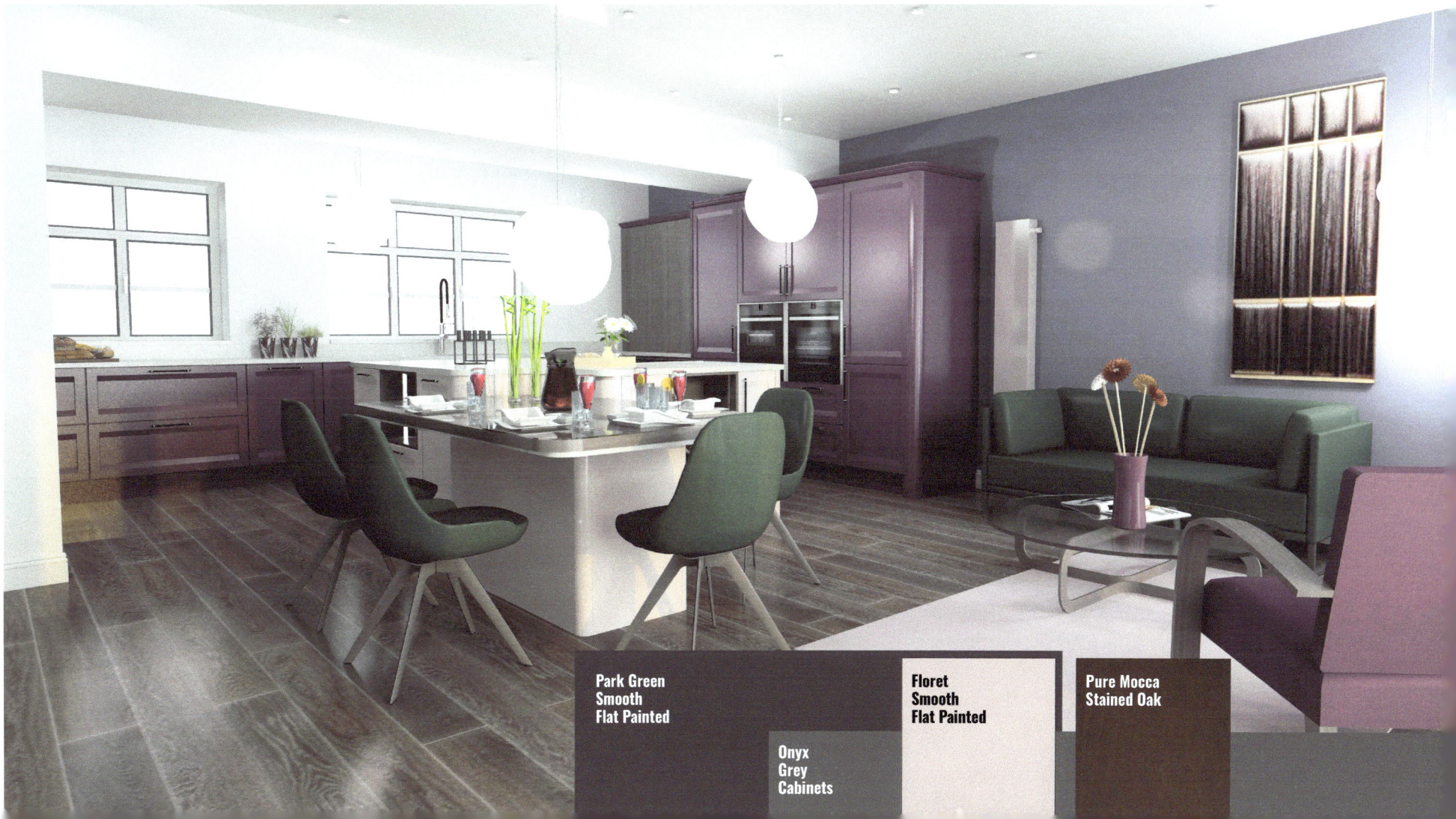

Park Green
Smooth
Flat Painted

Onyx
Grey
Cabinets

Floret
Smooth
Flat Painted

Pure Mocca
Stained Oak

Midnight Grey
Smooth
Flat Painted

Natural
Carini Walnut
Cabinets

Galaxy Blue
Smooth
Flat Painted

Pure
Oak

Brass
Handles

Extreme Restoration
Alternative 2
Project 011

Inspiration

SHAKER INSPIRED SIMPLICITY:
When Less in Design Becomes More in Function & Form

The essence of the Shaker Movement related to simplicity which translated as to their attitude and approach to furniture and design. The alternative scheme in this particular instance is an extrapolation of their philosophy. Form and function are important elements of all successful kitchens, this example aptly demonstrates that in many instances - less can well translate to more.

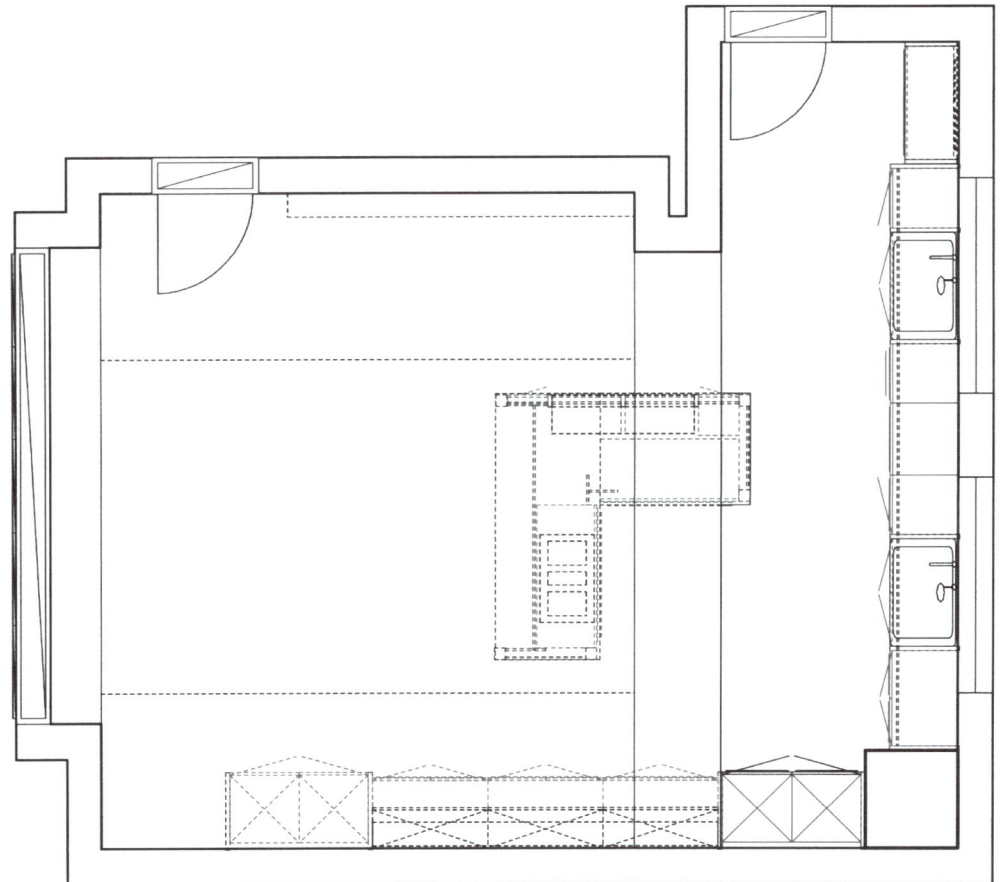

ISLAND INGENUITY

An interesting new build project in the North of Scotland provided a conundrum

An interesting new build project in the North of Scotland provided my long-time friend and colleague (Beverley) with a conundrum. How to go about incorporating all of her clients' many and varied requirements for their new kitchen into what was a generous expanse, but a testing challenge due to three sides of the available space involving floor-to-ceiling glazing.

The client's vision for the kitchen in their 'forever after' dream home was a blend of traditional and contemporary, with a large imposing island taking centre stage. Their new kitchen was to be incorporated into an offshoot from the main building, involving a double height room with a vaulted ceiling. Making the most of the vast amount of natural light and views was uppermost in their thoughts in relation to the orientation of both the house and kitchen.

Island Ingenuity
2010

Engaging with clients to gather as much information as possible is key in kitchen design

I've rather put the cart before the horse in the sense that prior to extracting this information from Beverley, I'd questioned her on her 'Technique/Practice' when embarking on a kitchen project. Her response was: "Engaging with clients to gather as much information as possible. Who they are, family circumstances and any specific requirements. A good chat over a coffee can reveal much and relaxes people; this encourages engagement and unlocks their aspirations. Taking time to understand one's clients can often lead to discussion in relation to new products and styles not previously thought about or considered. Developing their wish list is essential."

In this situation, the clients were both company directors with no children. Their dogs and cats were an important aspect of their lives. The kitchen was very much a joint venture in that both enjoyed cooking and entertaining. An important factor related to the provision of both formal and informal dining: the new kitchen was to be the central hub. In the client's own words to Beverley: "Our new kitchen must have pizazz, stand out and make a bold statement."

Developing the clients' wish list is essential in the design process

+ DOWNDRAFT EXTRACTION BUILT INTO FLOOR

+ KITCHEN DESIGNED IN SYMPATHY WITH UNDERFLOOR HEATING

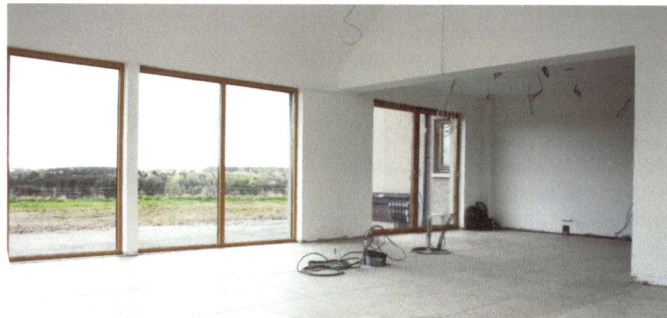

Their initial wish list covered a wide array of items: a single oven, combi steam oven, combi microwave, warming drawer, coffee machine, induction hob, wok hob, American fridge/freezer, dishwasher, wine cooler, 2 sinks, boiling hot water tap, mood lighting, music and TV. An extremely comprehensive list from clients who had done their homework.

As Beverley explained: "This trait is much welcomed, and makes my role as a kitchen designer easier."

Beverley made an important point. The clients had engaged her in the early stages of their project – this was long before they'd signed contracts with their timber frame manufacturer or builder. She explained how much easier it is if clients liaise with her as early on in their programme as possible; this particular undertaking was an excellent example.

The house required various areas to be addressed prior to pouring concrete. With the proposed kitchen, living and dining area being open-plan and with a double height vaulted ceiling, plus extensive floor to ceiling glazing, effective extraction was essential and required to be addressed at the foundation stage. The decision was made to install a powerful down draught extraction system requiring (as the image aptly demonstrates) a large ventilation pipe.

Under-floor heating requires the kitchen footprint to be available prior to commencement of the build, as this should not be installed beneath either the furniture or appliances. The provision of water, waste, gas and electrics also needs to be planned prior to installation of under-floor heating. These all highlight the necessity to ensure the kitchen design is made available early on in the project – retro-fitting any one of these aspects will prove expensive.

Engaging a kitchen designer early in the project, before contracts with builders, makes the process much smoother

Beverley made the point as to the importance of CAD drawings when working on a project such as this. With just a building plot and no house, it's difficult for clients to envisage the finished article. The 3D CAD drawings enabled her clients to truly engage and understand how their new kitchen would look and function.

This project goes back more than a decade, and Beverley's clients still love their kitchen – although as you will see from the more recent photography, they've updated the primary colour and added a contemporary wood burning stove, while the garden has been transformed. As Beverley explained: "Happy, satisfied clients make my job so worthwhile."

I leave you to peruse Beverley's handiwork: a job well done, and a first class example of how to tackle such a project.

Island Ingenuity
Alternative 1
Project 012

DUALITY IN DESIGN:
Balance & Symmetry
to the Fore

A total contrast to that which currently occupies
the house – more towards the contemporary,
but with a Shaker element incorporated into
the tall bank. The simple design and profile
of the double island, wet area to one side and
hob within the other and linked by a central
breakfast bar, is not only practical but ideal
in relation to utilising the available space.
A thought provoking substitute.

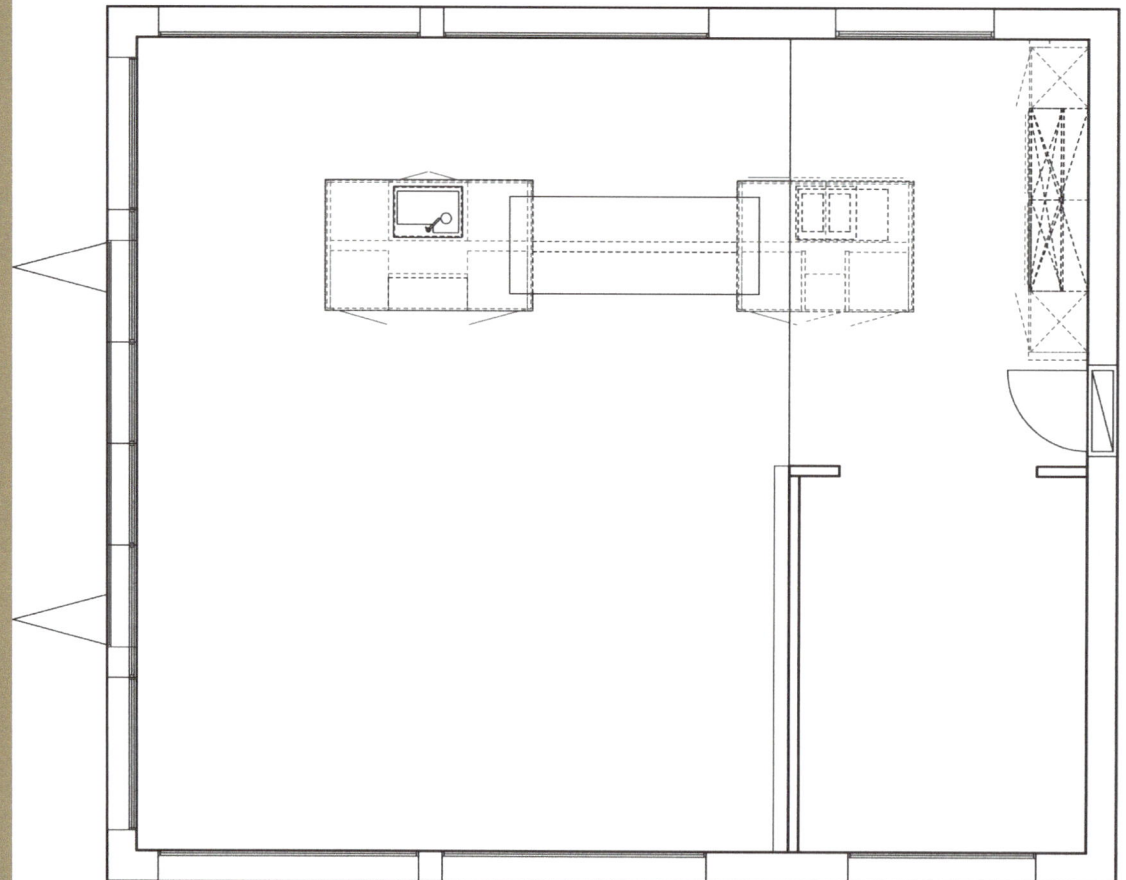

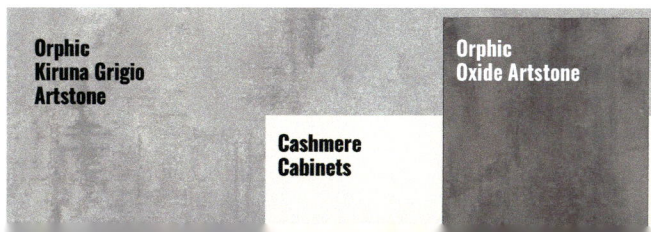

**Orphic
Kiruna Grigio
Artstone**

**Cashmere
Cabinets**

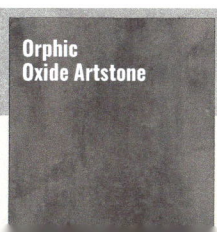

**Orphic
Oxide Artstone**

**Cashmere
Smooth
Flat Painted**

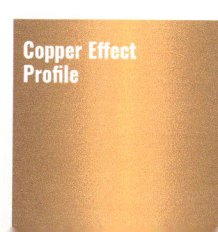

**Copper Effect
Profile**

Inky Green
Smooth
Flat Painted

Natural
Carini Walnut
Cabinets

Gransden Grey
Smooth
Flat Painted

Pure
Dark Grey
Stained Oak

Island Ingenuity
Alternative 2
Project 012

Inspiration

SOPHISTICATION & FINESSE:
Generated via Incorporation of Design & Flair

A further alternative to what is a spectacular space surrounded on three sides by full height glass. What was at first perceived a conundrum, proving to be a boon – with the vast island floating in a sea of daylight! The scale of the island with its raised and curved breakfast bar, along with incorporation of novel open shelving makes for a bold statement. The tall bank with butler's pantry no less so.

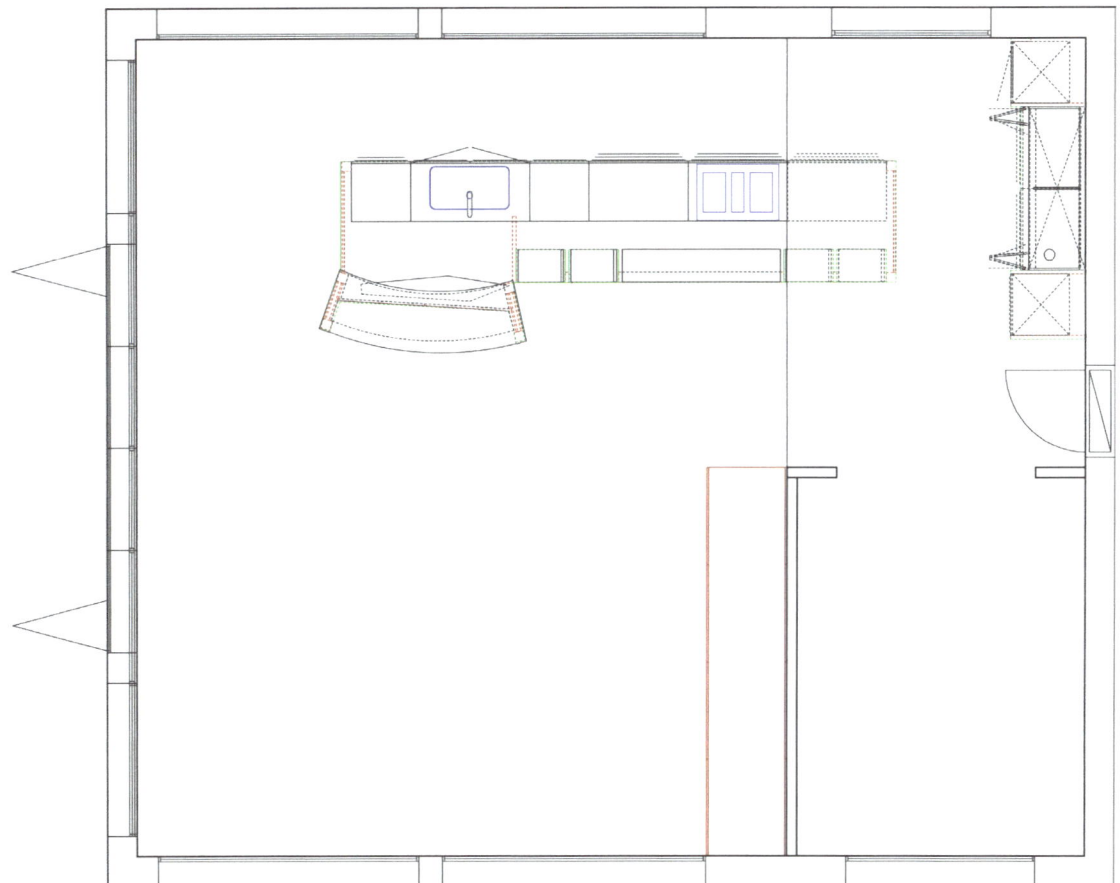

DESIGN DIVERGENCE

Jenna, a kitchen designer, has a unique background with a degree in Kitchen Design from Bucks University

The dictionary definition of 'Diverge/Divergence' is to take a different course or proceed in an alternative direction. Extremely apt in relation to this particular project and the importance of the designer establishing and understanding a client's individual needs, requirements and expectations for their new kitchen.

Jenna is a long-time colleague with an interesting background in relation to the design-led kitchen world. She, along with a group of young, enlightened and enthusiastic students, signed up for the inaugural FDA Kitchen Design Degree at Bucks University and graduated with distinction in 2017. As you will learn, this had an influence and bearing on her receiving the commission for this particular project.

During the clients' initial visit to her studio in the North of Scotland, Jenna learned that they were very much at an early stage in relation to sourcing a new kitchen; first and foremost they were looking for inspiration. Initial thoughts related to a new kitchen utilising the existing space. Their one major ambition related to installing bi-fold doors in place of the existing conventional windows, to provide direct access as well as views in relation to their much-prized garden.

Jenna discovered the clients' preference for a contemporary kitchen design with a connection to the outside space & an adjoining snug

Jenna also established they were keen to have a more contemporary design with not only better connection to the outside space, but also the adjoining snug and the possibility of incorporating a wood burning stove. The couple were keen to create a kitchen where they could entertain family and friends. There was an existing separate formal dining room, and thus a desire to include a more casual dining space – possibly along with a breakfast bar.

I asked Jenna as to her relationship with the clients and how they'd sought out her company. She answered: "The clients were looking for a design-led kitchen specialist and had done their research. They liked the fact we were a small team who pride ourselves on great design and customer service. They'd also been recommended by a family member. My recent completion of the FDA Kitchen Design Degree proved of interest; we built a bond and trust very quickly."

There's an interesting insight to be gained from Jenna as to how the client/designer relationship developed: "They were excited, inspired and appreciative of how I challenged their initial ideas and questioned some of their thinking. They wanted the best possible design in relation to function, but also with the wow factor. They were receptive as to my suggestions, although it took a few visits and presentations to come around to certain aspects of this."

Jenna explained: "The initial presentation took the clients by surprise, and their reaction to the sink not being in front of the window took a while for them to get their heads around. By demonstrating what could be gained by moving the sink (enabling the inclusion of a wood-burning stove), they were shocked at how well the space flowed and the size of island they could have." The benefits of 3D CAD drawings were aptly demonstrated in this instance.

Design Divergence
2019

I'm always interested as to the influence a designer brings to bear in relation to the design/architecture and layout of a project. In this instance, Jenna believed she impacted this as follows: "Once we'd established the format of the furniture and the sink was to be in the island, it made sense to drop the kitchen 'sink' window to the floor, providing space to install a wood burning stove." As can be seen, making these changes enhanced the kitchen layout.

The clients' original preference had been for a contemporary white kitchen, in total contrast to their existing model. Once again, Jenna influenced this decision: "When it came to colour and material choice, I encouraged them to add contrasting grey tones via wood and concrete textures alongside the use of staggered furniture heights and depths – providing a more interesting and individual look to the kitchen."

Further design touches Jenna introduced to the project related to the seamless Corian work surfaces (ideal due to the scale of the island), mirrors in the wall furniture reflecting the garden, and false plasterboard walls to create depth and interest. Underfloor heating was utilised, negating the need for wall space for radiators.

The kitchen is a real statement piece, and as Jenna explained: "The realisation from my clients when it clicked that this could actually be their kitchen really stood out for me, as it was beyond anything they'd originally envisaged."

Initially favouring
a contemporary white kitchen,
the clients were influenced by Jenna to add contrasting grey tones & textures

Winter Finch
Grained
Painted

Natural
Carini Walnut
Cabinets

Orphic
Expressions
Mid Intaglio
Vetta

Pure Mocca
Stained Oak

Design Divergence
Alternative 1
Project 013

Inspiration

BOLD, BRAVE, & ECLECTIC:
A Lesson in Combining Contrasting Elements

The utilisation of false walls and a variety of different styles combine to create something out of the ordinary. The separation of cooking, refrigeration and storage into three distinct zones on the rear wall proves highly effective. The wet area, preparation and breakfast bar incorporated into the island, all ably bond together via a bold palette of colours, materials, and contrasting constituent parts.

Design Divergence
Alternative 2
Project 013

Inspiration

DIVERSE DIRECTION:
A Further Example
as to the Breadth
of Options

The design focus in this instance more Classic but without compromise when it comes to function – a vital element of all successful kitchens. No matter your chosen style, practicality can and should be incorporated. An interesting combination: - Chimney breast and mantle, tall appliance bank flanked by book shelves, refrigeration, plus a prominent centre island featuring quadrants and breakfast bar.

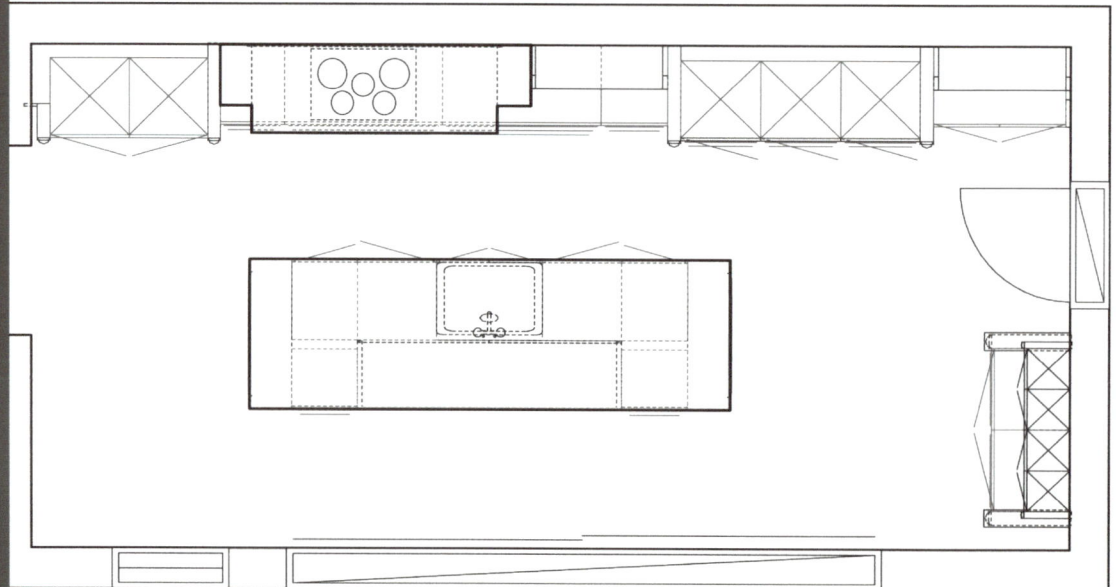

Special
Smooth
Flat Painted

Natural
Hamilton Oak
Cabinets

Poached Plum
Smooth
Flat Painted

Pure
Oak

Abstract
Expressions
Pewter
Halifax Oak

POIGNANT

My choice of title for this particular case-study deserves an explanation. Mike, a long-time friend and colleague, succumbed to cancer – hence this being a 'Poignant Project'. Mike, during his far too brief time on this Earth, made an impact in many ways – but his passion for kitchen design and creativity is what I wish to explore via this project.

PROJECT

Poignant Project
2017

Unlike the other case-studies, I was not in a position to interview Mike. So I've had to approach this in a different manner. I was well aware of the project, as it featured in Callerton's website and brochure. It also appeared as a kitchen case-study in a magazine (March 2018). But the major input and inspiration has come via Mike's clients, as well as a number of his colleagues whom I'd like to acknowledge and thank for all of their help and assistance.

The magazine article began: "Creativity, flexibility, and adaptability are said to be the hallmarks of a good designer, along with a host of other traits. So the clients made the right choice appointing Mike Grant to assist them in creating their dream kitchen." I believe this helps set the scene for an unusual project.

Creativity, flexibility, & adaptability are said to be the hallmarks of a good designer... So the owners made the right choice appointing Mike Grant to assist them in creating their dream kitchen

Over the years I was lucky enough to meet a number of Mike's clients, either at kitchen studio functions or attending photography shoots. So I was well aware of his modus operandi, which first and foremost related to making friends with his clients. I'm sure Mike would not be offended if I was to say that his approach was relaxed (time was never of the essence), ensuring he'd fully examined all aspects and possibilities of a design; it was his way of working.

Mike's enthusiasm and passion for design, as well as pushing the boundaries, were at the heart of how he went about all projects, and this was an excellent example. Forming a relationship and bond with a client is something I've always subscribed to. Mike was an excellent exponent of this, and well understood the benefits of such.

Sinead (Mike's client) recounted: "We moved into our house in September 2014 and the kitchen was small, dark and at the rear of the house. Our aspirations involved a much bigger open-plan kitchen, and one that was good for entertaining family and friends." She also recalled that their first meeting with Mike related to a set of plans extending the living room into a kitchen living/dining space, which involved dispensing with the old kitchen.

However, after consultation between client, architect and designer, it was decided a better option was to knock two rooms at the side of the house into one and further extend the area to provide a new zone framed by floor-to-ceiling glass to take in the view of the impressive garden and lake. The finished article totally vindicates this volte face.

Sinead explained: "Mike's company had been highly recommended to us by friends. When we first spoke with him, he proved to be good at listening to what we wanted, but also gave us new ideas and suggestions which we took on board to create the magnificent design we have to this day."

"Our aim was to create a spacious kitchen and dining area that flowed seamlessly from the front door and hallway. The brief to Mike was for a minimalist look with lightly-coloured cabinetry and walnut accoutrements to complement the traditional features found elsewhere in the house, such as our curved walnut staircase."

Mike's approach was relaxed, ensuring he'd fully examined all aspects & possibilities of a design; it was his way of working

+ PROPOSED DEVELOPMENT

+ EXISTING PROPERTY

The concept of the twin islands...allowed maximum movement throughout the area without splitting the room in two

"The concept of the twin islands related to a kitchen we had seen on a trip to Ireland and something we felt would be an effective layout, allowing maximum movement throughout the area without splitting the room in two, which we believed a single island would have done. Mike readily took on board the concept and further developed this."

One such aspect was eloquently explained by Craig (Sinead's husband): "The step up on the first island was originally put forward as a method of hiding clutter when entering the room, as well as providing a cupboard to house our crystal. This now operates as the unofficial meeting/standing place, as well as the official cocktail-making station and referred to as the 'bar'. I suspect Mike knew this would be the case – but was wise enough not to sell it as such."

Sinead summed it up: "We actually love it all; each part has a purpose and meets our daily requirements. We spend much time in the kitchen, and it is definitely a great social space for family and friends."
One final accolade to Mike's craft and legacy: his colleagues are currently working on a further project for the family – within their grounds.

**Dried Lawn
Smooth
Flat Painted**

**Pigeon Grey
Smooth
Flat Painted**

**Pure
Mocca
Stained Oak**

**Natural
Carini Walnut
Cabinets**

Poignant Project
Alternative 1
Project 014

Inspiration

ISLAND MASTERCLASS:
From Twin Island to an Unusual Option

Could come straight from MasterChef and for individuals wishing to strut their culinary skills to those around them. U-shaped islands require space and this project possesses the opportunity to demonstrate such. The eclectic mix of materials and styles adds depth and interest. An aspect deserving of a mention: - The built-in corner seating arrangement and table complement the kitchen.

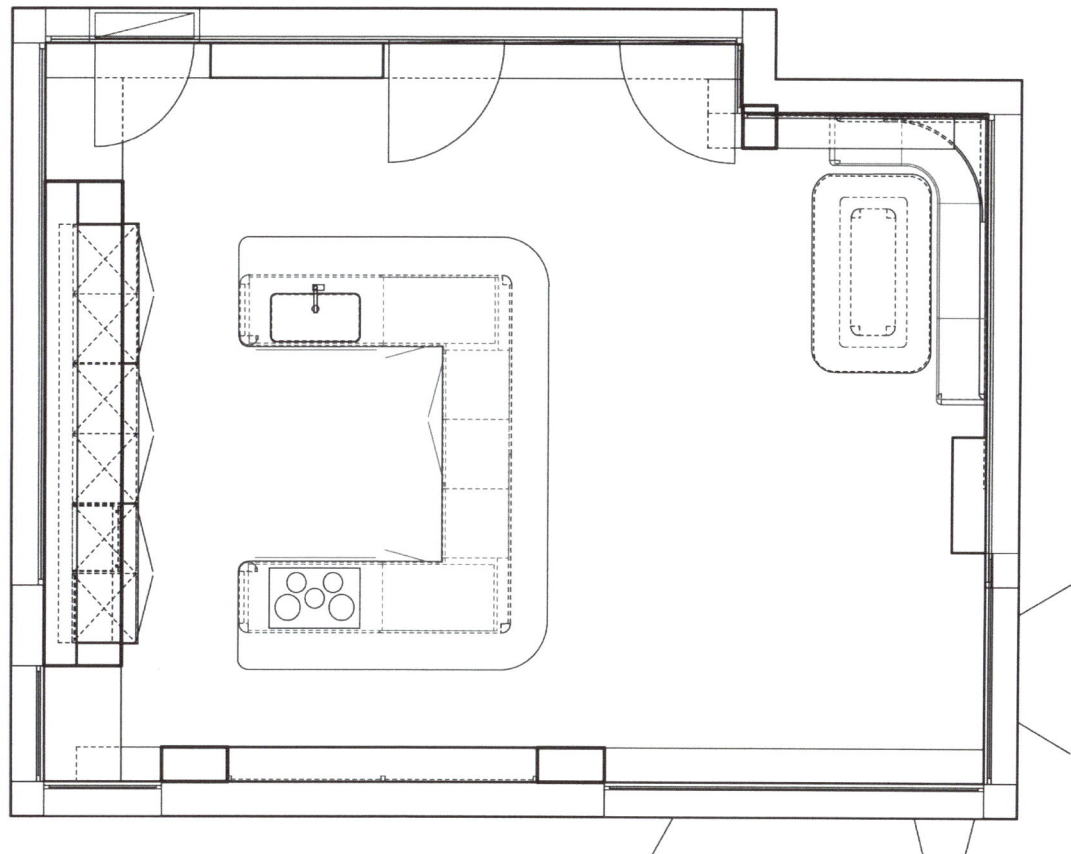

Poignant Project
Alternative 2
Project 014

Inspiration

DEVELOPING THE THEME:
An L-shape Alternative Adds to the Options

An L-shaped island with lower-level breakfast-bar arrangement provides a further island concept and option. Once more could work for those with a culinary exhibitionist streak. A totally functional and practical layout separating the cooking element from other functions. The glazed dresser/pantry and refrigeration bank demonstrates excellent use of the alcove - supplying practical storage solutions.

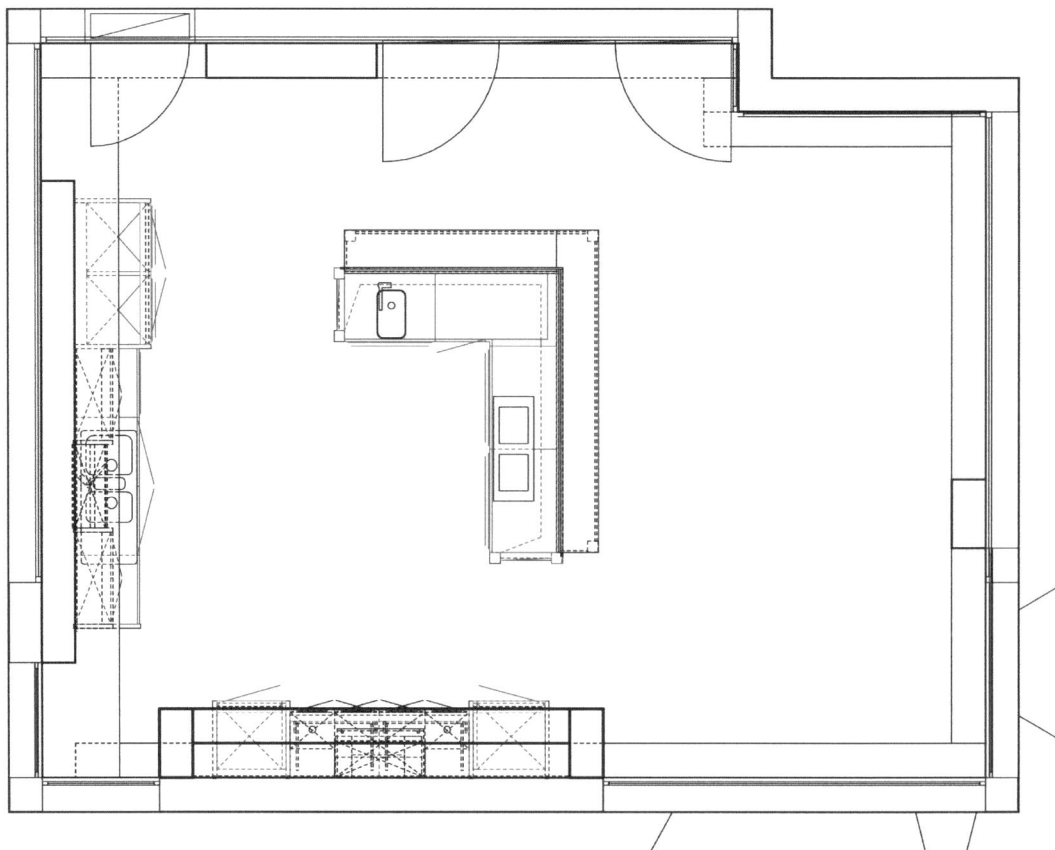

Wilkins Grey
Smooth
Flat Painted

**Kaisersberg
Oak
Cabinets**

Porcelain
Smooth
Flat Painted

Midnight Grey
Smooth
Flat Painted

PIÈCE DE RÈSISTANCE

This particular project epitomises why engaging a design-led kitchen specialist when embarking on the creation of your 'Dream Kitchen' pays dividends.

Although this particular individual's skill and ability surpasses both me and many of my compatriots, Phil is a long-time friend and we've worked together for more than quarter of a century.

Pièce de Rèsistance
2022

Project 015

"We always carry out a full or partial survey of the house... This provides an overview of the existing layout and how all the various areas work & interact with one another."

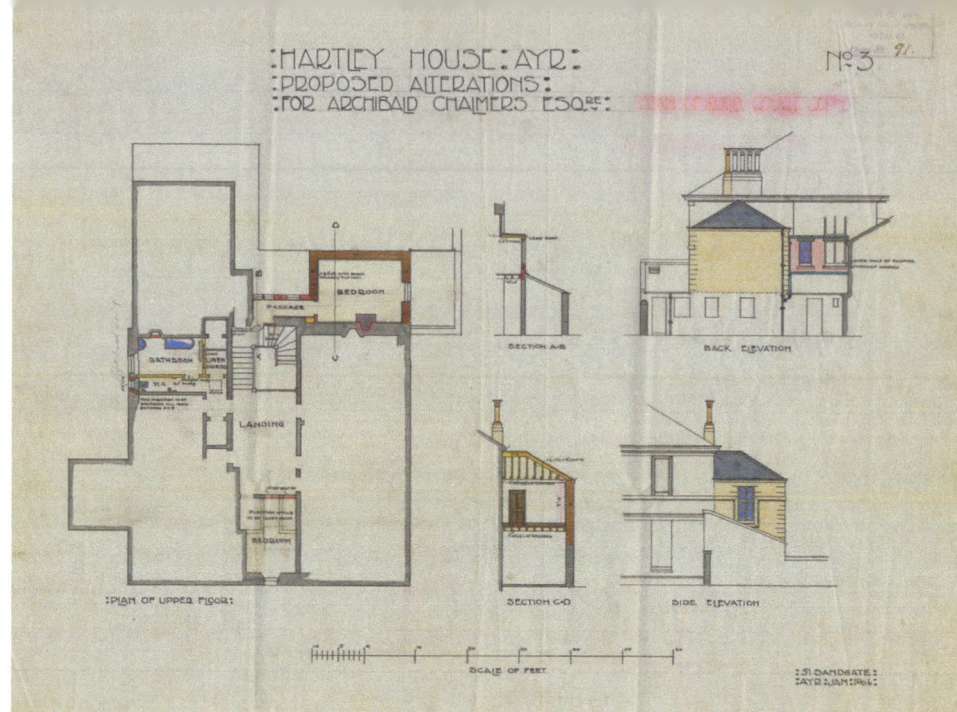

Like me, Phil describes himself as an academic reject and employs a fairly unique approach, as I hope to demonstrate. His answer to my first question sets the scene: "When working on a project, what course of action do you follow?"

"We always carry out a full or partial survey of the house, whether in relation to the ground or subsequent floors. This provides an overview of the existing layout and how all the various areas work and interact with one another – which ensures we maximise the full use and benefits of the property." The next comment is typical Phil:

"Adding a kitchen is easy – but its relationship with and interaction to other rooms and how a family group utilises, or wishes to use, their home is important. Just presenting a kitchen layout fails to provide the full story; without engagement with the wider picture, it would be easy to miss opportunities to maximise a property's potential."

This project aptly demonstrates just how far Phil will go in relation to ensuring he has explored all eventualities. I'm possibly getting ahead of myself in that first I should relate the relationship between client and designer.

Phil explained: "We had an extremely close relationship, as we'd worked together on their previous property. I also undertook the project management of other areas and aspects of the renovation of the new house, hence an excellent rapport from an early stage." My next question demonstrates the breadth of Phil's involvement: "In relation to the design/architecture/layout of the property, did you have an influence or impact on this?"

"Yes. We wanted to create a modern, vibrant living space that reflected the architecture of the house by utilising a classic Shaker door with a modern handleless twist. This tied in with the vaulted double height ceilings with American cassette style detail. We also rebuilt the end gable in reclaimed stone from redundant outbuildings, and added bi-fold doors to the same. Incorporation of the old wine cellar and recessed wine cabinets were further touches."

This project aptly demonstrates just how far Phil will go in relation to ensuring he has explored all eventualities

+ EXISTING KITCHEN

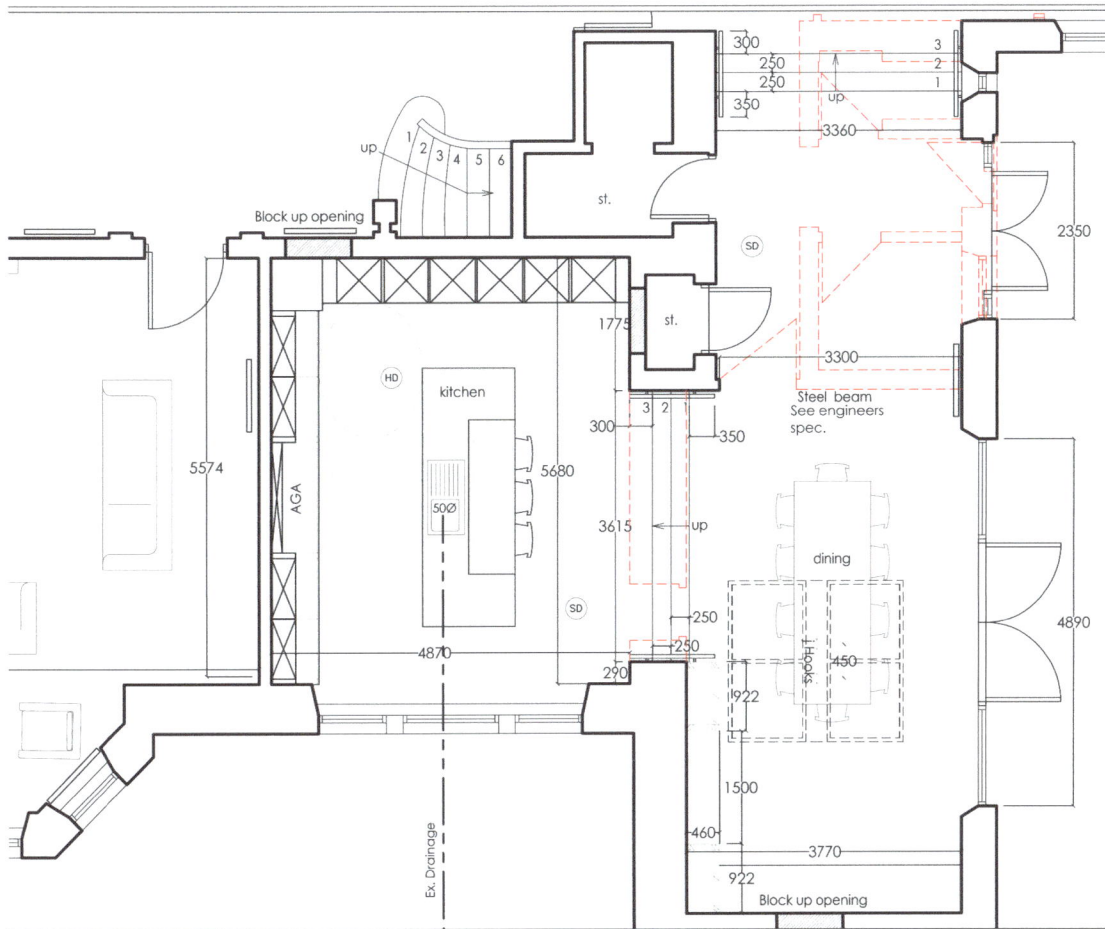

+ PROPOSED REDEVELOPMENT

Phil revealed a key discovery:

"The original extension at the rear was built in 1909 and hadn't been constructed as designed... On investigation... these showed the anomaly which assisted us in our case with the planning officer"

What I learnt a little later in proceedings shows this to be something of an understatement when Phil explained: "The original extension at the rear was built in 1909 and hadn't been constructed as designed, this being for staff accommodation. On investigation and utilising the Freedom of Information Act to access the plans from that time, these showed the anomaly which assisted us in our case with the planning officer and allowance of alterations."

It is worth adding that the property is listed as well as being in a conservation area. Another snippet I learnt from Phil was that the original kitchen was landlocked within the house, with only a single side window. The two-storey extension added around 1909 was the reason for this. The transformation is even more amazing when taking this into account.

An aspect which has been discussed throughout 'Insights' relates to CAD (computer aided design) imagery. On discussing this with Phil, he explained: "CAD and 3D imagery were critical elements in developing the project."

+ SUBSTANTIAL INTERIOR BUILDING WORK

The title of the case-study 'Pièce de Rèsistance' is apt, as the dictionary definition relates to: The best or most exciting thing – best item in a group – outstanding item – often the last in a series. I leave you to decide from the photography of the completed project which of these best suits and describes the project.

There are so many outstanding aspects of Phil's design that deserve mention: The simplicity of the hybrid kitchen is complemented by the detail in the dining area with its bi-fold doors, the high windows from the original second floor, the exquisite ceiling detail, the steps down from the kitchen, and recessed wine cabinets. A pure masterclass in design.

A couple of quotes from Phil as to what gave him the most satisfaction: "An invite to my client's fiftieth, and seeing so many people enjoy the house." On asking the clients for feedback as to their kitchen, their reply was: "Our first night ensconced in our new kitchen finished at 4:00 in the morning, as we were totally bowled over with final result."

The simplicity of the hybrid kitchen is complemented by the detail in the dining area with its bi-fold doors, the high windows from the original second floor, the exquisite ceiling detail, the steps down from the kitchen & recessed wine cabinets

Pièce de Rèsistance
Alternative 1
Project 015

CHANGE OF DIRECTION: Crossover/Hybrid Transitions to Classic

A very different genre to Phil's design and highlights the disparate nature of how individual clients wish their new dream kitchen to look and perform. The inclusion of an iconic Aga tends to be a decision clients make prior to engaging a Design-led Kitchen Specialist. Add the imposing chimney breast, dressers, and island with an unusual curved breakfast-bar – all combine to tick a classic box.

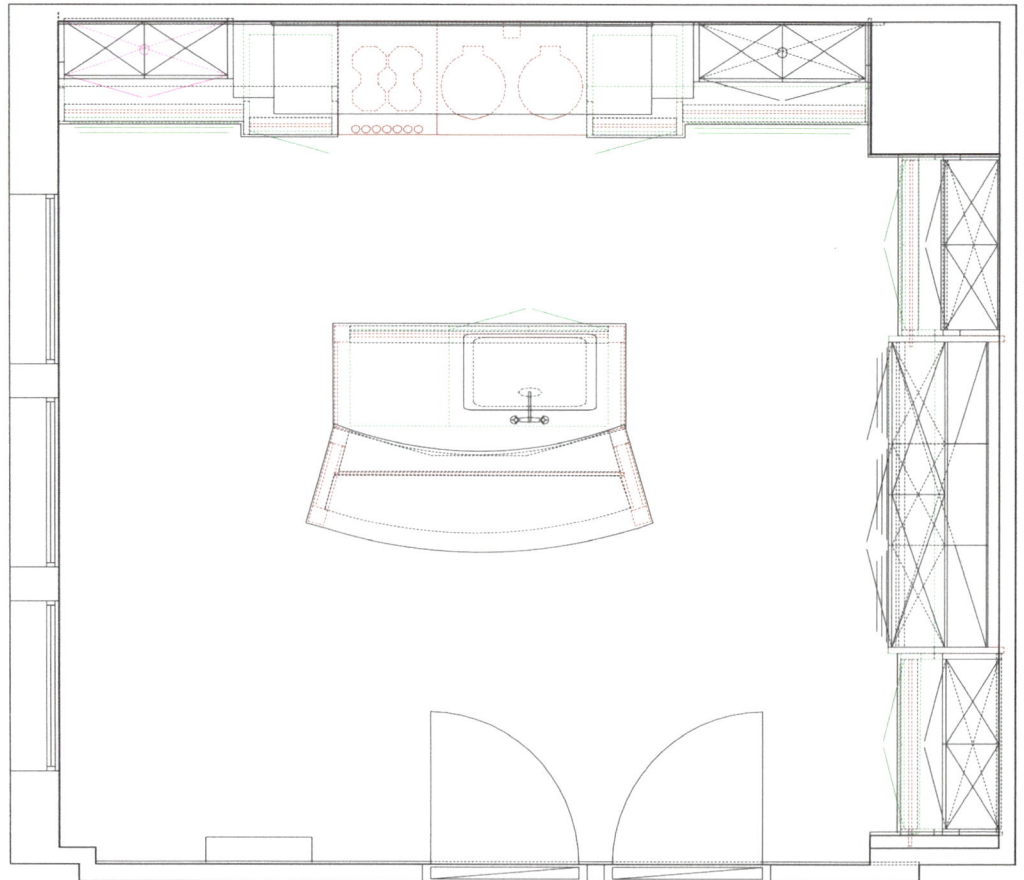

North Grey
Smooth
Flat Painted

Light Grey
Cabinets

Special
Smooth
Flat Painted

Abstract
Expressions
Natural
Halifax Oak

Walnut
5% Sheen

Natural
Carini Walnut
Cabinets

Monza
Matt
Reed Green

Pure
Dark Grey
Stained Oak

Pièce de Rèsistance

Alternative 2
Project 015

Inspiration

OPPOSITES ATTRACT:
A Further & Opposing Possibility

A geometric theme is embraced in this modernist design – emphasising the breadth of options available to clients when provided with a blank sheet of paper. The tall elements are flanked by different heights, depths, open furniture, doored cabinetry and interspersed with a palette of contrasting materials: - Wood, paint, stone and ceramic tiles – all combine to shout contemporary.

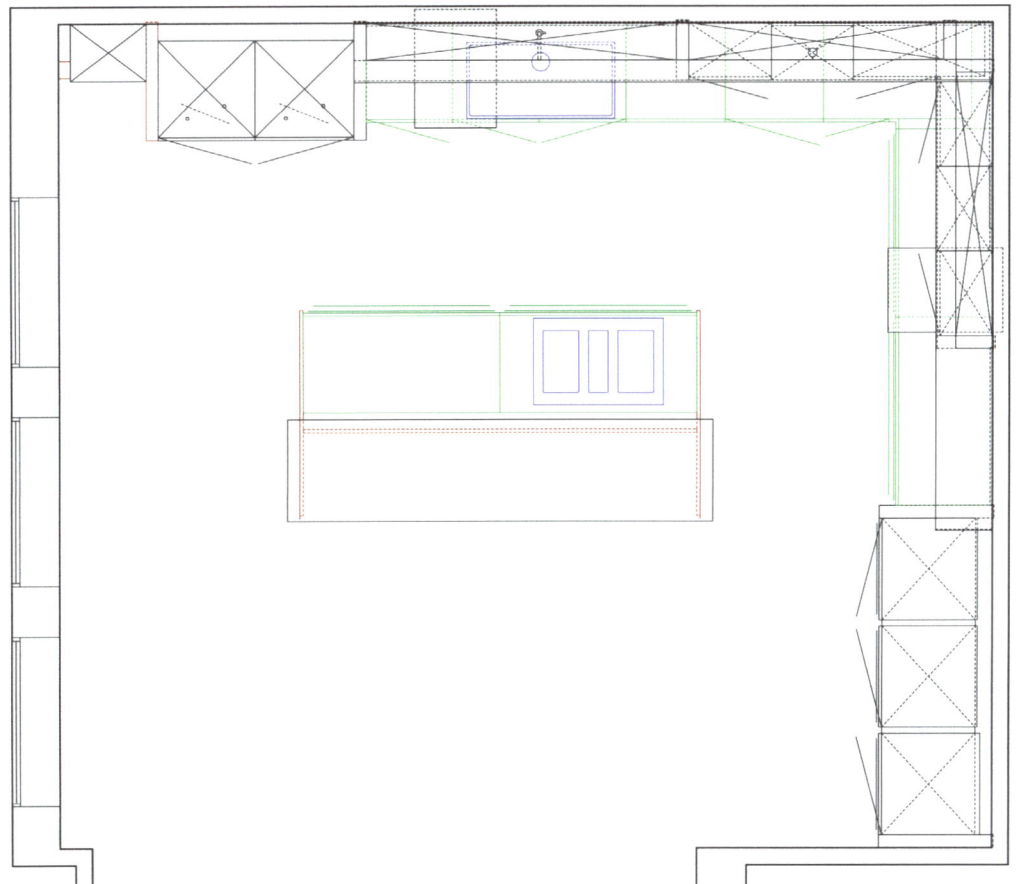

The title of this particular case-study is extremely apt –

not only from a kitchen perspective, but more so the new-build house within which this resides, and the way they come together in total harmony. Mandy, a much-respected Callerton colleague, developed the kitchen design in conjunction with her client to empathise with the house layout

This was best demonstrated by Mandy's answer as to my question: "Explain your client's initial vision, thoughts and intention for their particular project." Her response helps to explain much:

"My client had a vision of how she wanted the kitchen and living spaces to meld with one another. The ground floor was to have an ergonomic flow with as few doors as possible, but with each area's purpose defined and identifiable. There was an emphasis on being streamlined, and with a focus on aesthetics. A large walk-in larder catering for storage was required and had to be readily accessible from the kitchen. The outside space was to flow with the internal layout, with an external dining area incorporated. The build was to focus around modern/contemporary natural materials."

GRAND DESIGN

Mandy added: "I became involved in the project from the point of the plans being passed, but prior to the build commencing. This was to ensure my client's vision was achievable within the defined space, but without having to make any adjustments to the plans." An eminently sensible approach to follow when engaged in such a project.

I'm fascinated about the relationships that develop between designer and client, and asked Mandy how theirs evolved. "The relationship built up between the client and ourselves became one of trust and friendship. They visited us on numerous occasions, always happy to sit and chat – to discuss options and budget (which was blown very early on in proceedings). They were happy to be guided through the process and receptive to advice and knowledge."

My own personal experience and belief regarding the importance of trust and relationships (gained over 40+ years) has been emphasised time and again via all the diverse projects incorporated within 'Insights'.

In this instance, this was aptly demonstrated when asking Mandy: "Do you have any memorable quotes from your clients relating to the project or relationship with them?" Her answer was: "The client would ask me to clarify her decisions and choices and conclude with, 'And what would you do Mandy?' followed by, 'I'm happy to go with your choices'."

Grand Design 2022

"My client had the idea of a dark colour, utilising industrial materials"

"From the outset, I like to build a good relationship, get the client to trust my knowledge and assure them that by working together we can achieve the dream."

Throughout my 'Insights' venture, I've probed each designer as to their way of going about a project. Mandy's response was: "From the outset, I like to build a good relationship, get the client to trust my knowledge and assure them that by working together we can achieve the dream. I always take on board what they want: this is paramount, and if not achievable never to be disparaged. My goal is to inspire via design and wherever possible incorporate their vision."

In relation to the kitchen design, I was keen to understand what aspects of the architecture influenced Mandy.

"Alongside the open-plan nature of the layout, there were two particular elements that stood out and influenced me: the first being the central fireplace which opened onto both areas, the kitchen and snug. The positioning of this was critical to the ergonomics of the kitchen. The second was the extremely high rear wall within the kitchen, and my client's wish for everything to be to hand. Luckily, in this instance, it was agreed the rule could be broken."

An aspect that's been repeatedly mentioned throughout 'Insights' relates to the importance of 3D CAD imagery. Mandy was no different, and stated: "This aspect was paramount for my client in that visualising the kitchen layout and look would have been difficult without CAD. It greatly assisted in helping them to make product choices, and to understand how the kitchen would both look and function in relation to the rest of the house."

With regard to product choices, Mandy proffered that she'd brought a modicum of influence to bear: "My client had the idea of a dark colour, utilising industrial materials. Developing a colour palette to demonstrate such helped in making their final decisions." As you can see, these were excellent choices, and so effective alongside the architecture of the house.

Mandy's final statement in relation to what stood out for her was: "The whole project was a pleasure to work on; the clients were brilliant, and watching the building come to life – and being part of this – was very special."

Dried Lawn Grained Painted

Natural Hamilton Oak Cabinets

Ink Green Grained Painted

Brass Handles

Grand Design
Alternative 1
Project 016

Inspiration

VOLTE FACE:
Transition from
High Tech to a
Traditional Genre

Individuality in style is the pre-requisite of each client and their particular vision for their dream kitchen. In this case from opposing factions - contemporary to traditional emphasises the broad spectrum of available options. A variety of elements and detail sets the scene: - Painted furniture, Aga, extra-height cabinetry, Belfast sink, in-line chimney canopy, plus the unusual island detail.

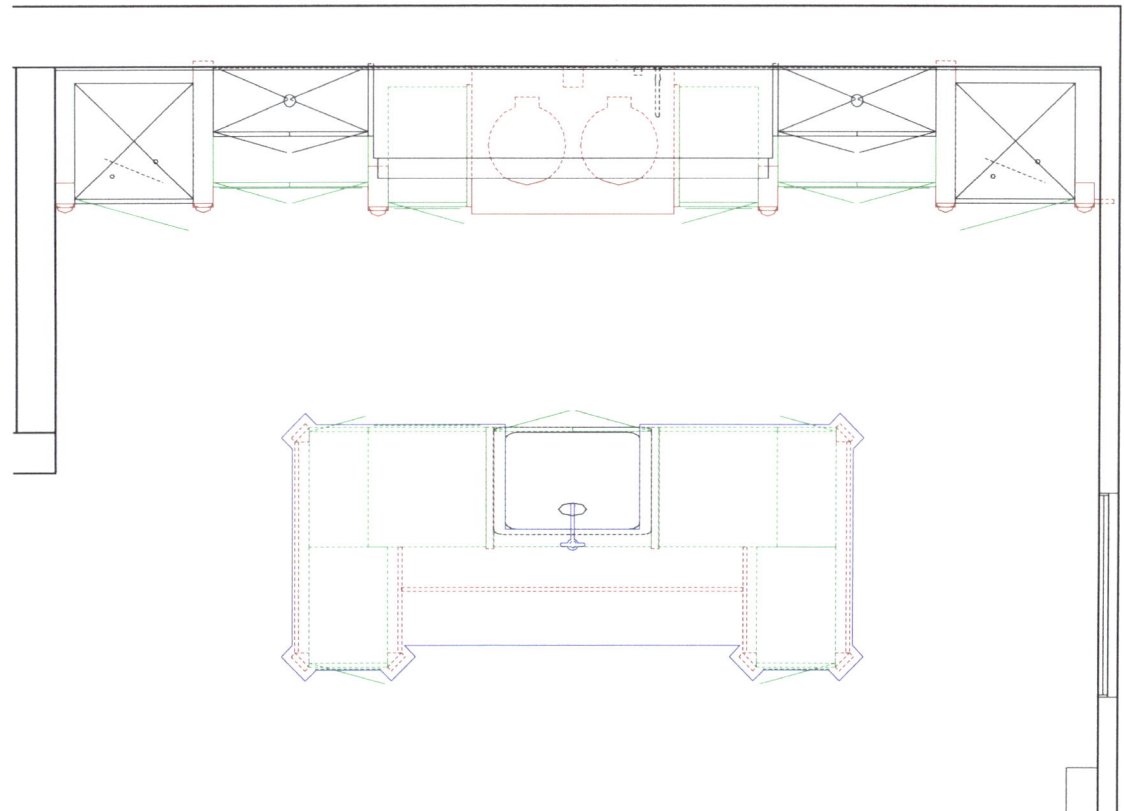

Grand Design
Alternative 2

BOLD AS BRASS:
Appeal to those with an Extravagant & Exuberant Nature?

An eclectic mix of colours, materials and styles makes for a bold statement. An example that going 'off the beaten track' and exploring avenues beyond normal boundaries – may well be the answer for those with an adventurous spirit. Conventional Shaker painted (in a bright vivid colour) vie with Industrial high tech materials, alongside retro features incorporating both – truly thought-provoking.

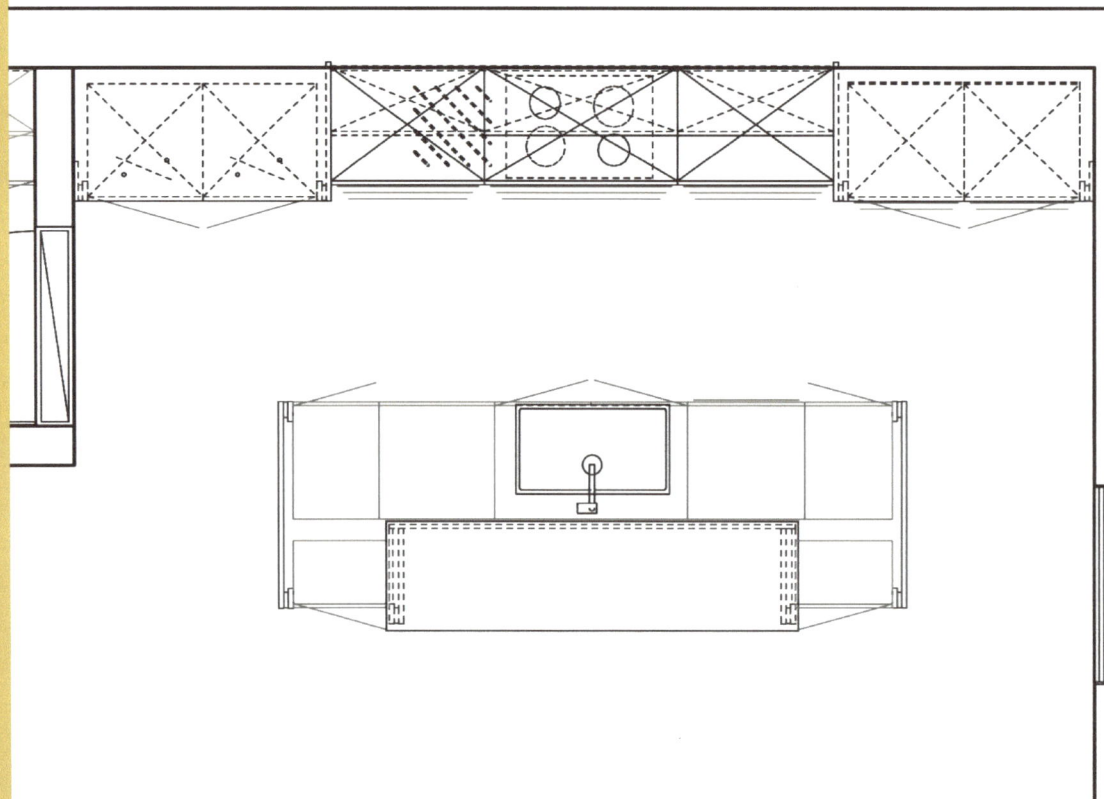

Netherton Grained Painted

Grey Textile Cabinets

Abstract Expressions Black Gold Metal Slate

Valencia Gloss Black

MINIMALIST
MARVEL

The clients' initial vision for their new-build project required this to be minimalist – hence the title. This snippet of information came via Angela and Jeremy (a husband and wife team) who've been a Callerton dealership ever since the inception of their business, and based in a beautiful Cotswolds town. Angela's answer to my question in relation to explaining their clients' initial vision, thoughts and intentions for their particular project was as follows:

"The house is situated in the centre of a wonderful garden which is dominated by a huge, extremely old Cedar tree. Our clients' vision related to a kitchen, living and dining area with a vaulted ceiling and glazing to three walls, enabling them to enjoy panoramic views of the garden. They wanted the house to be minimalist, decorated exclusively in pure white, with accent colours in key furnishings to provide the home with an expansive feeling of space and light."

My further question as to how the clients had come across them, and regarding the development of their relationship, provides an additional insight: "The clients had spent months travelling all over the country trying to find the right kitchen, and were on their way back from Liverpool when they happened to pass our showroom. We hit it off straight away and believe once they'd seen our initial draft design, were confident we understood them and they trusted us."

"Our clients' vision related to a kitchen, living & dining area with a vaulted ceiling & glazing to three walls, enabling them to enjoy panoramic views of the garden."

Minimalist Marvel
2015

Backed up by the answer to my question in relation to memorable quotes from their clients: "We described our requirements to Angela and Jeremy, they got it straight away. They knew exactly what we wanted. I think even from the very first drawing produced, we altered very little other than a few tweaks. Nothing was too much trouble. Looking at lots of kitchens made us realise what we did and didn't like, so – on seeing this one – we knew it was right."

"Looking at lots of kitchens made us realise what we did and didn't like, so – on seeing this one – we knew it was right."

Angela and Jeremy's approach when working on a project helps to explain this:

"We believe the brief is the most important part of the process, engaging the clients and entering their world to understand their family dynamics: how they live, cook, entertain, relax, and their vision for what impact they want the new space to have on their lives. We carry out a site visit even on a new build, to get a feel of the surroundings and where the property sits within this. We take photos of the property and garden, art or family photos on display, and import these into our designs. We want our presentation to look like their kitchen, not a design concept."

"We described our requirements to Angela & Jeremy, they got it straight away. They knew exactly what we wanted."

I should explain that as this was a new build project, Angela and Jeremy were working from architects' drawings, which neatly links to my question to Angela in relation to the importance of CAD software when working on a project such as this. Angela's response was:

"Without question, it is an invaluable tool – particularly regards open-plan and especially when the space does not as yet exist, and vital when trying to demonstrate a concept the client has not seen before. It proved invaluable in this instance, as our clients could see 3D imagery of how the kitchen would look and function within their new home."

A particular aspect in relation to this was the clients' desire for the kitchen to appear minimalist and to look as if it was floating. By raising the sink run and the media centre off the floor and utilising mirror plinth on the island, they were able to achieve this. Angela stating: "The CAD imagery was a boon in demonstrating this effect." As mentioned earlier, the clients had very specific views in relation to style and the use of colour as an accent. Angela added to this: "We very much followed the initial brief, but influenced this in relation to the appliance choices, work surfaces and also introduced Zebrano as a contrast, which our clients instantly loved." The imagery of the finished kitchen demonstrates how effective Angela and Jeremy were in bringing the various elements together.

An unusual and unexpected answer to my final question, bearing in mind that this project goes back more than a decade: "Tell me anything in relation to the project that stood out for you." Angela reminded me this was the first time they'd incorporated open shelving above the ovens: a concept she'd seen in Austria and mentioned, subsequently on attending an exhibition, that she was surprised and delighted to see we had incorporated this into our display and range.

I believe this to be a masterclass in engaging with clients and surpassing the aims and ambitions for their kitchen. What appears simple and minimalist is in truth far more nuanced than that, achieving an outstanding result.

Minimalist Marvel
Alternative 1
Project 017

Inspiration

REFINED GRANDEUR:
Alternative Perspective Regards Form & Function

A change in layout and look can change perception – refined grandeur replaces bold contemporary. The 'L' shape design generates an opportunity to alter operational aspects of the kitchen. Form and function are highly personal and the juxtaposition of the incumbent kitchen and the alternative - an excellent demonstration of such. Creating a kitchen to satisfy an individual's needs is sacrosanct.

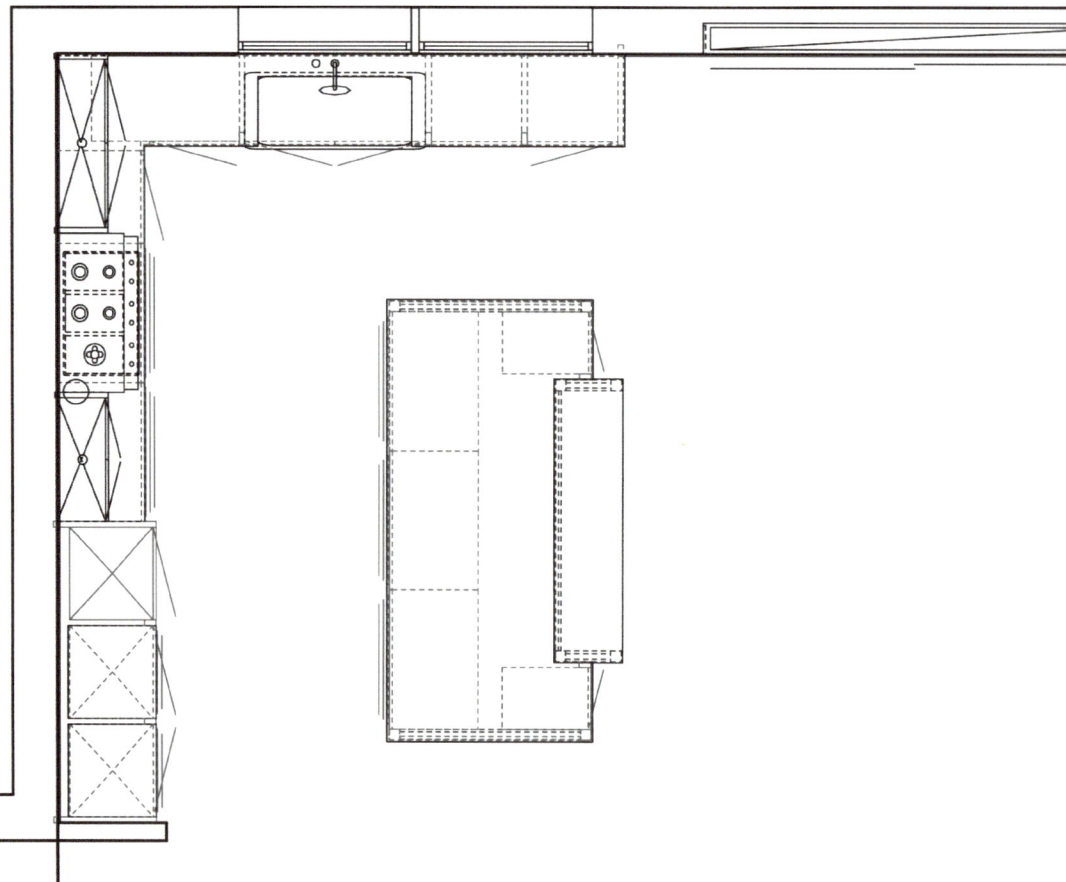

Deep White
Smooth
Flat Painted

Sea Kelp
Smooth
Flat Painted

Natural
Carini Walnut
Cabinets

Monza
Matt
Black

Onyx
Grey
Cabinets

Pure
Mink
Stained Oak

Minimalist Marvel
Alternative 2
Project 017

Inspiration

MATERIAL CHANGE:
Subtle Alterations to Elements & Aspects of the Original

Initial inspection possibly creates the false impression the design is similar to the original layout – but closer inspection demonstrates this to be a misnomer. The change of colour likely to produce a polarised reaction – and possibly disguises how much has altered. The island incorporating the elegant breakfast bar, and the nuanced detail of the tall appliance bank are worth investigating.

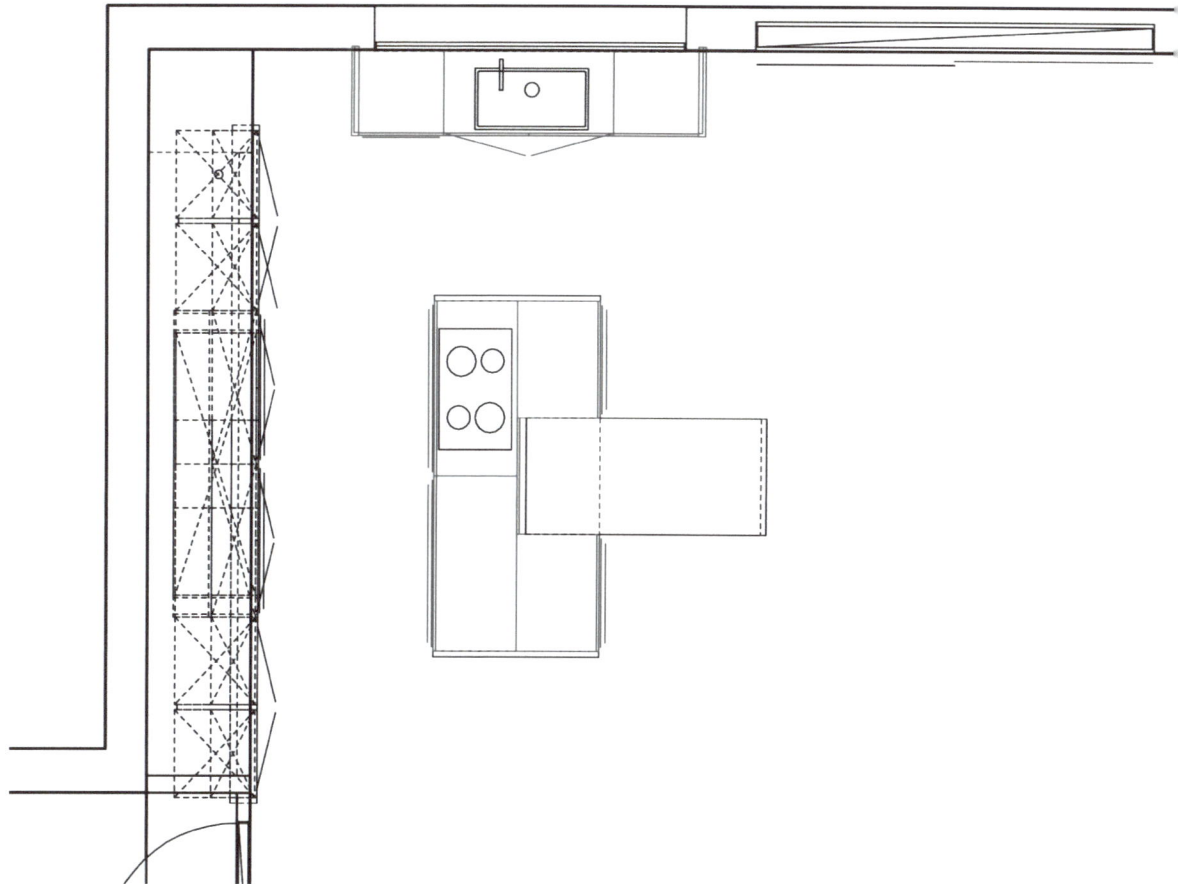

SALUTARY STYLE

An interesting but apt title to this case-study. Salutary appears in the Oxford English dictionary as: Producing good effects – beneficial. As the owner of this kitchen is someone who styles homes for leading estate agents in the North of England, 'Salutary Style' seemed fitting. Her skill and ability were ably demonstrated via imagery of the finished project.

Michelle is a long-time friend and colleague of mine, and the designer in this particular instance. On enquiring as to what category she would place the project and what her client's initial vision was for this, Michelle explained:

"An extension and renovation of an existing building was required with the emphasis on creating a vibrant open-plan living space incorporating kitchen, living and dining. My client's occupation ensured they had a definite perception of the overall feel required of the space, of which the kitchen was to form the focal point. The design was to possess a timeless, classic air in relation to colours and materials, but with a modern streamlined look."

Michelle expanded on this: "The property was undergoing a complete renovation with the aim of creating a future-proof house for when the couple retire (although this is probably a long way off for a very busy couple). This led to certain specific requirements regards accessibility and layout." An admirable and extremely sensible approach when embarking on such a project. Multi-generational kitchens and forward planning are a passion of mine.

The design was to possess a timeless, classic air in relation to colours & materials, but with a modern streamlined look

Salutary Style
2023
Project 018

On enquiring as to what stage in proceedings Michelle became involved, she replied: "After the architect and clients had finalised the dimensions of the extension in which the kitchen would reside, with my client being clear she wanted the kitchen to be positioned so it connected with the dining and living spaces so whilst working in the kitchen she could engage with the whole space." A clear vision and understanding of requirements is always a boon for us designers.

I was interested as to how Michelle saw the relationship between the client and herself, given she was dealing with someone from a design background. The answer was interesting: "We clicked on a personal level, and believe I understood the overall look the client was hoping to achieve. In turn, she felt she'd found a kindred spirit with the same tastes and values in relation to design." Creating a trust and bond makes the experience special for all parties.

This was demonstrated by Michelle's follow up: "In the main, I developed the design with my client. However, towards the end of the process – when we'd more or less finalised everything – this had to go before her partner. The nice aspect being that as we were on the same wavelength, she trusted me and his approval was forthcoming."

Creating a trust & makes the experience special for all parties

A clear vision & understanding of requirements is always a boon for us designers

I wondered whether Michelle had deviated from her normal practice of establishing the client's 'Aims, Needs and Ambitions' for their new kitchen, given she was a design professional. The answer being "No," followed by:

"I take a lot of time to discuss what they want to achieve as regards style, layout, storage, appliances, etc. I find asking my clients to spend time creating a Pinterest board is invaluable; the process allows them to explore and identify images that appeal, and generates a starting point for discussion and exploration, as I followed in this case."

In relation to influencing the design, architecture and layout of the property, Michelle pointed out: "Most aspects had been set prior to my engagement, these having involved the architect and planning authorities. One area where I was able to offer input and advice related to the addition and positioning of the roof-lights. Availability of CAD imagery assisted in this, as well as helping to demonstrate how their new kitchen would both look and function."

As Michelle was dealing with a design professional, I was intrigued as to whether or not she influenced her client's choices in relation to style, colour, worktops, appliances, etc. Her answer was: "My client had a palette of colours and textures she was working with in relation to the property as a whole. I proposed shades and materials that complemented these. The subtle Dekton concrete work surface I suggested was loved by my client, but not all members of the family – fortunately the end result proved my client and me correct, and is now universally approved of."

Michelle's one area of disagreement related to the freestanding fridge/freezer – she proposed that this be integrated, but was overruled by the client. This was rightly their prerogative. I don't believe this impacts the overall look or function of the kitchen. Another excellent example of a kitchen case-study – and as to the client's styling, this deserves praise.

Monza
Matt
Graphite

Onyx
Grey
Cabinets

Orphic
Aged Oak
Grigio

Salutary Style
Alternative 1
Project 018

Inspiration

SIMPLICITY TO THE FORE:
A Clear-Cut Modernist Approach

A no frills, minimalist contemporary approach, diametrically opposed to that of Michelle's Shaker-inspired design. Beauty is in the eye of the beholder – a well-worn phrase but emphasises the importance of designing to satisfy the end client's needs and requirements. Gathering together all the information and detail and interpreting such to exceed a client's expectation being the goal.

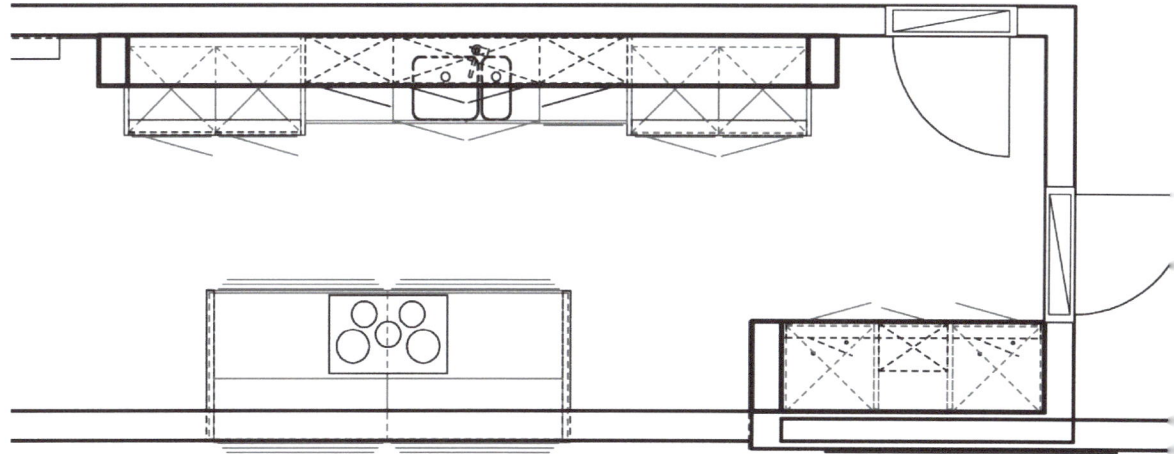

Salutary Style
Alternative 2
Project 018

Inspiration

DECO INSPIRED:
Radiused Features Versus Square Edged Profiles

Balance and symmetry with the incorporation of curves duly alters the aesthetics and feel. Radiused features enable a distinctive approach and look in relation to the centre island and its breakfast-bar arrangement, via stepping aspects forward and back. A couple of details worth noting relate to the treatment of the cornice, as well as the double radius of the plinth detail; small but highly effective.

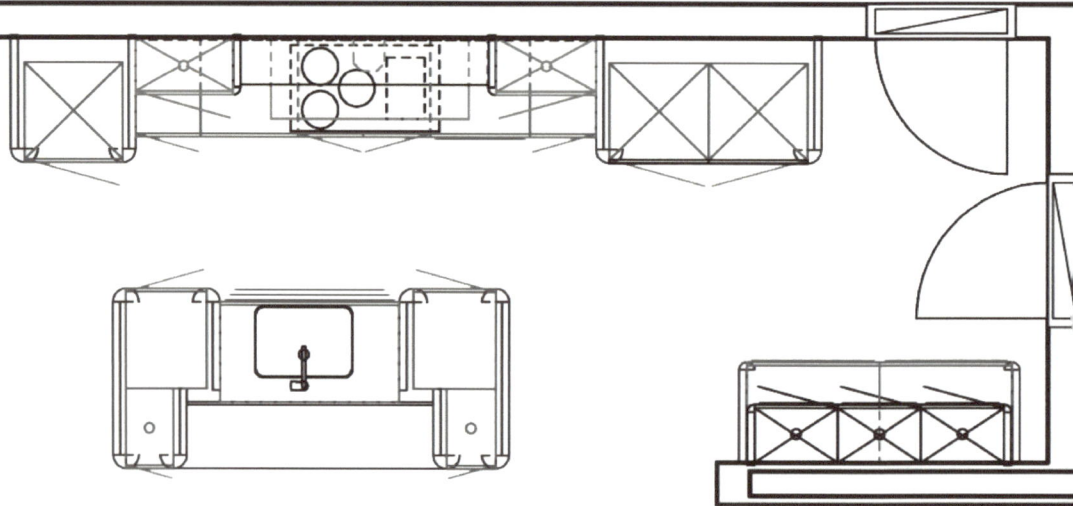

**Inky Green
Smooth
Flat Painted**

**Brass Effect
Profile**

**Natural
Carini Walnut
Cabinets**

PARTY

CEN-TRAL

This particular case-study involved extending an existing property (circa 1930s) with the clients' criteria wish list incorporating a number of novel priorities and features from the start.
My long-time colleague and top-notch kitchen designer (Andrew from the West Midlands) enlightened me as to these, and how he went about the project.

Party Central
2020

Andrew explains: "Our sociable clients love entertaining and were set on a soft industrial vibe, with a modern twist. They were keen that the kitchen was not just filled with furniture, and expressed a love of symmetry. Their dream dining table had been shortlisted, and we utilised this as a starting point. They also desired the incorporation of a brick accent." I also gleaned that Andrew's involvement commenced after planning permission was received for the new extension.

Given what I was learning about the project, I was curious as to how the relationship between client and designer developed. Andrew clarified: "They were nervous to begin with, as they'd been to other kitchen studios but hadn't been inspired or enthused. I believe their default position was an expectation of disappointment. But after presenting our initial scheme, the relationship quickly developed into one of trust and mutual understanding."

I was interested as to how Andrew goes about establishing a client's 'Aims, Needs and Ambitions' for their new kitchen. His answer was both interesting and enlightening: "I want them to feel they are my one and only client. To listen intently (two ears, one mouth) is crucial, as it enables me to understand how they currently live and how they want to live going forward. From this, I can develop solutions to ensure such are incorporated into the proposed scheme."

Our sociable clients love entertaining & were set on a soft industrial vibe, with a modern twist

"The light available through the Crittall doors, & also the roof lanterns, meant we could be bold with colour"

Andrew's memorable quote regarding his clients highlights the importance of his previous statement: "I don't believe they ever used the phrase 'Party Animals,' but it was made clear on several occasions (at an early stage) that the new extension was to be utilised for entertaining and parties!" Not your everyday design request and priority, but great to receive feedback as to a client's wishes and desires and to ensure these are built into the project.

I'm always interested as to whether the designer has influenced or impacted the architecture or layout of the property, or whether any existing features within the building have done so.

In this instance, Andrew suggested: "The refurbishment involved a full-width extension to the rear of the property, incorporating three sets of Crittall doors overlooking the mature gardens (with pool). The Crittall glazing worked beautifully as a launch point for creating that all-important soft industrial vibe and, together with some huge roof lanterns, helped to set the stage for an amazing sociable/ entertaining space incorporating kitchen, living and dining."

The answer to my question as to whether or not Andrew influenced the client's choices in relation to style/colours/appliances/ worktops etc. highlights the benefits of engaging an able designer:

"Yes, definitely. The light available through the Crittall doors, and also the roof lanterns, meant we could be bold with colour. Inky Green was selected with a slim framed Shaker door. We felt the need for a simple worktop finish as a contrast, and in terms of finish and composition something that would not vie with the brick and floor textures. Glacier white Corian (50mm) was ultimately chosen, which contrasts beautifully with the brass handleless profile."

As to what aspect gave Andrew the most satisfaction, the answer was: "How the scheme integrates with the rest of the property and both the existing and new ancillary furniture and furnishings. For example, the brushed brass handleless profile coordinates with the finish of the pendant lights, also the Buster & Punch switch-plates. A simple dark oak floating shelf is a nod to the floor finish, and ties the tall housings neatly together whilst helping to frame the texture of the brick wall, with the LED up-lights behind the Corian upstand adding to the overall effect."

In relation to the title of this particular case-study, 'Party Central,' it is worth pointing out the feature making use of the disused chimney breast. (Designers love utilising such spaces creatively.) Andrew's clients have a spectacular collection of alcoholic beverages which required a home, and are now housed in the midi height glazed cabinetry.

A point worth recording as to Andrew's motivation in relation to his role: "The ability and gift to be able to contribute to making a real impact on the way people live and further the enjoyment of their homes."

Party Central

Alternative 1
Project 019

Inspiration

MATERIAL REVOLUTION:
Creates a Totally Different Ambiance

Similarities in layout to the present kitchen, but a change of materials generates a different experience. Flat panelled contemporary timber-effect doors combined with vertical handleless profiles – a total contrast to the incumbent Shaker painted furniture. Other standout elements relate to: - Modernist glazed cabinetry, imposing island worksurfaces, eclectic colour palette – a masterclass.

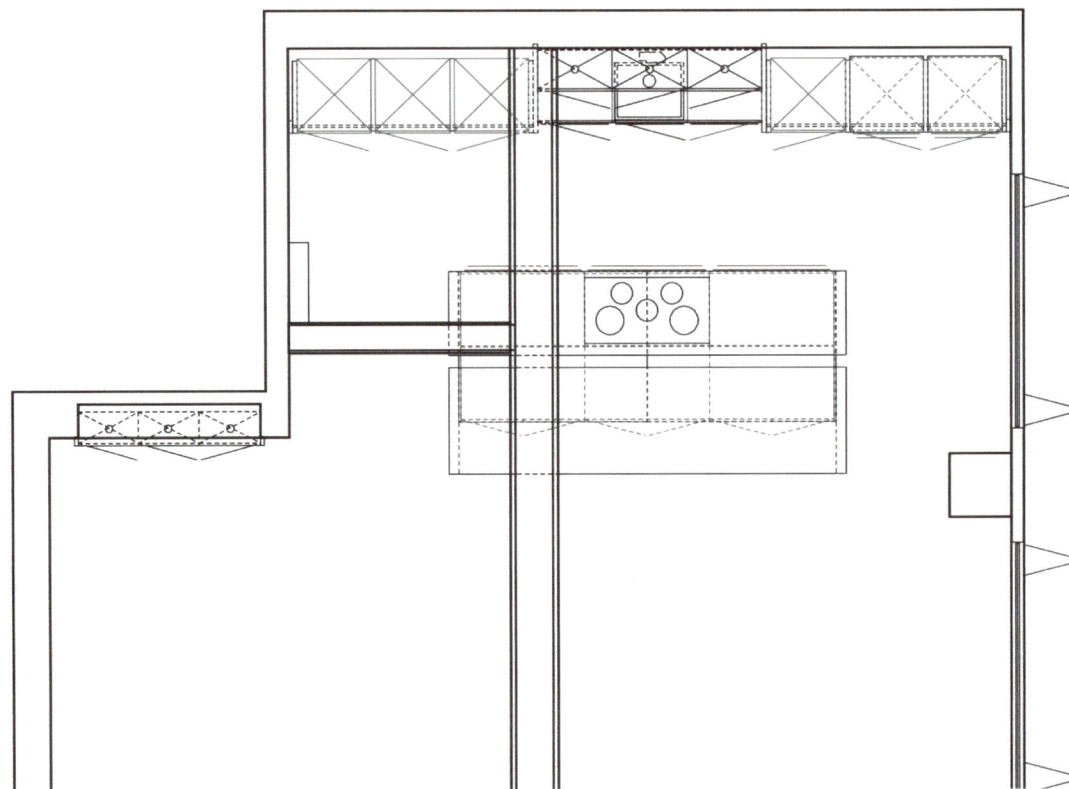

Abstract
Expressions
Pewter
Halifax Oak

Onyx
Grey
Cabinets

Orphic
Tigerwood
Nero

Black
Smoked
Glass

Party Central
Alternative 2
Project 019

Inspiration

AGELESS & MASTERFUL:
Much Loved Classic & Timeless Genus

The style, layout and effect could not be more different than the previous two examples. This the epitome of traditional/classic kitchen design which rightfully retains a broad following. The ubiquitous Aga, chimney breast and mantle, allied with an unusual island layout incorporating a breakfast bar - help to demonstrate the diversity of options, given the identical floor space.

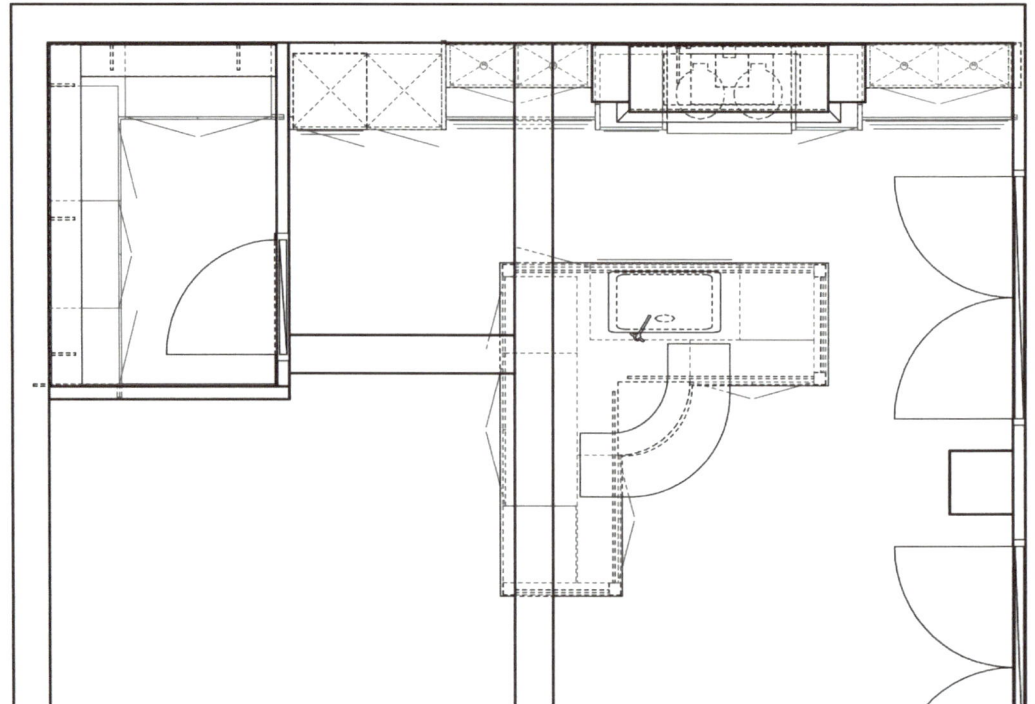

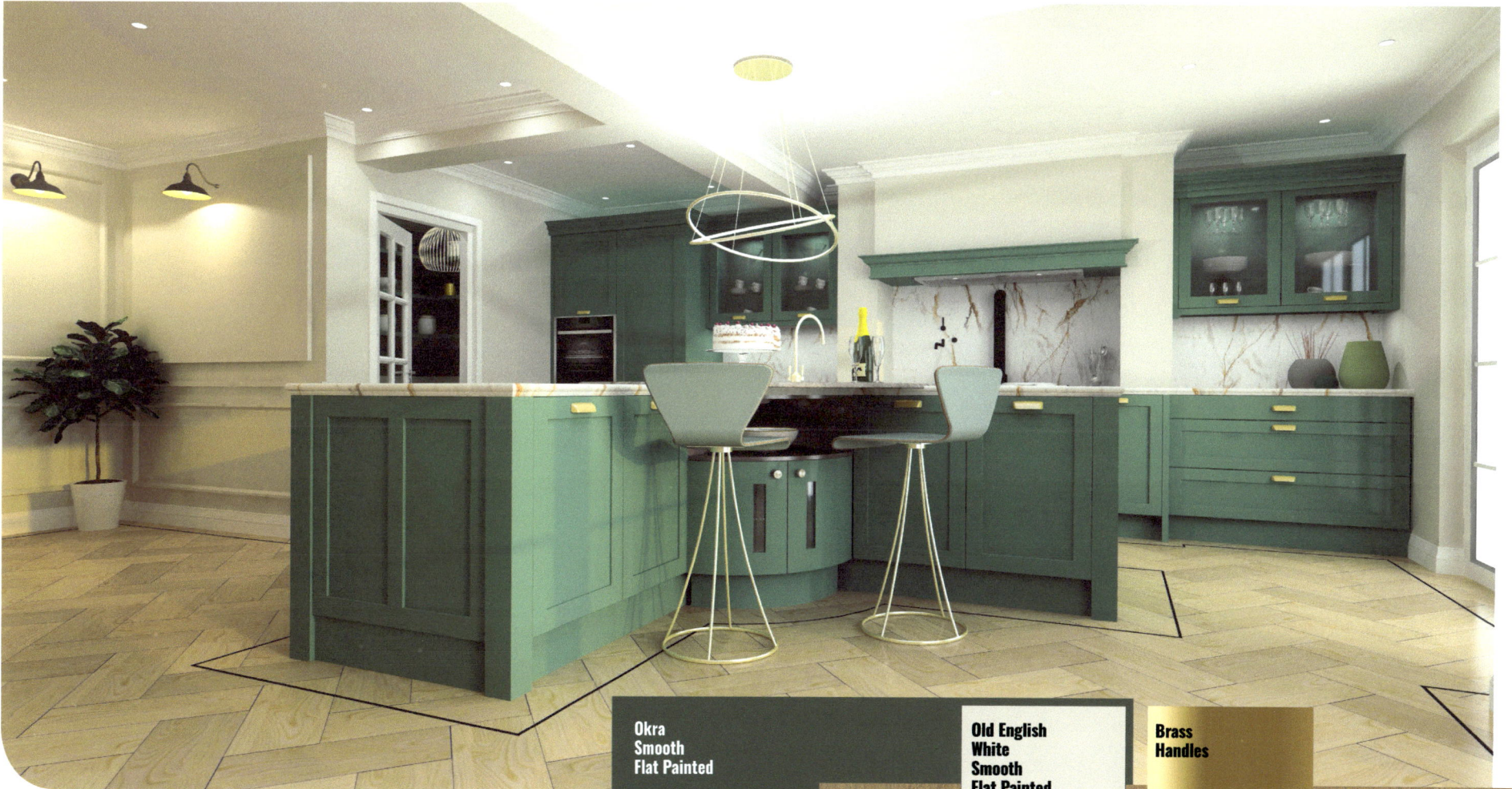

Okra
Smooth
Flat Painted

Natural
Hamilton Oak
Cabinets

Old English
White
Smooth
Flat Painted

Brass
Handles

PERFECT SITUATION

Emily, the designer of this impressive project, is second generation – having taken over the business from her Mum.

Ours is a special working relationship going back many decades.
The apprentice now becoming the master, as will be demonstrated.
Emily's explanation as to her clients thoughts and intentions for their project helps to set the scene:

"The aim was to create a hardworking kitchen area that would be the entertaining hub of the house for a very sociable Australian family who love to entertain. They wanted an island as large as possible (comfortably seating six), as this was what they'd been used to in Oz. The owner was a very keen cook, hence the kitchen was required to be extremely practical, with the ability to maintain a good degree of clear work surfaces. Having always dreamt of an Aga – this being the starting point for the appliances – timeless in style and bold in colour was high on their agenda. And capitalising on the beautiful lakeside vista was paramount." I was interested as to how Emily goes about establishing all this information. Her answer was:

"To begin with, it is always to listen and to ask plenty of questions. And then listen some more. I repeatedly hear clients tell me they don't feel they've been heard by other companies. Once I've earned their trust is when I can start to influence and add real value." Wise words, and a demonstration of Emily's professional approach.

Perfect Situation
2016

Project 020

"The turning point was on presentation of the initial design, where they saw the idea of a hidden entrance to the pantry"

The answer to my next question, "Tell me about the relationship you built-up/developed with your clients as the project proceeded," helps to further demonstrate Emily's mastery of her craft:

"Inevitably to begin with there is an element of restraint on the client's side, no matter how highly recommended you have come. The turning point was on presentation of the initial design, where they saw the idea of a hidden entrance to the pantry incorporated into the project – something which automatically opened up possibilities and gave the kitchen the scale they craved. Once trust is built and the client can see you truly add value and know what you're talking about, in this instance I

could almost visibly see these highly ambitious professionals let a barrier down."

As ever, I'm rather putting the cart before the horse in that it's important to understand at what stage Emily came to be involved in the project. It turns out this was fairly early on, once planning permission had been sought for the new extension and the builder appointed. The relationship with architects and builders is an aspect which interests me, and as ever Emily's answer was enlightening: "It was very good. I always work hard to make sure it is so, and they see me and my team as part of theirs. We've since gone on to carry out further projects with both the architect and the builder."

The kitchen element blends so well not only with the internal living space, but also the external elements such as the deck, garden & lake

In relation to questioning Emily's influence on her clients' choices reference style/colours/appliance/worktops etc., her response was: "My client had fallen in love with a Fired Earth colour for the furniture, and I knew she hankered after a black Aga. Having been able to demonstrate these through rendered CAD imagery (and I did agree they would work), those elements were pre-set. She was keen on a contrasting island work surface (as seen in our showroom), and given the size it needed to be a large enough slab to make the 3.2 x 1.6m island work. I took my client to the granite importer to source a suitable slab, and we both agreed on Cosmic Black to tie in with the black Aga."

An aspect of the project that Emily highlighted, and a further demonstration of her ingenuity:

"We had an issue with the extraction for the island hob. Initially the builder confirmed that with an external motor, the extractor could be flush with the ceiling. This turned out not to be the case! A minor panic ensued as the client did not want anything hanging down, nor a boxed section to house the extraction. The issue I believe in the end gave the kitchen an added wow factor. The solution involved boxing down to mirror the exact size of the island and cladding the underside with mirrors. We also echoed this by inserting a mirror in the bridging unit above the Aga."

I believe the best way to conclude this outstanding kitchen case-study is via the imagery of the finished project. It possesses so many attributes: the kitchen element blends so well not only with the internal living space, but also the external elements such as the deck, garden and lake – a masterclass in approaching such a venture.

I leave the last word to Emily as to her personal motivation: "To co-create a stunning heart to my clients' homes, and leave them with a cherished, forever-kitchen in which to make memories."

Perfect Situation
Alternative 1
Project 020

Inspiration

ART-DECO INSPIRATION:
A past Era's Influence ref Style & Fashion

The 1920's/30's Art-Deco movement created a whole new style and philosophy in relation to design. This instance involves aspects harking back to that era. The multiple curved elements incorporated into the island design add a sense of theatre. Callerton embrace the concept of 'Turning Dreams to Reality' – this project helps to demonstrate frontiers and norms are there to be questioned.

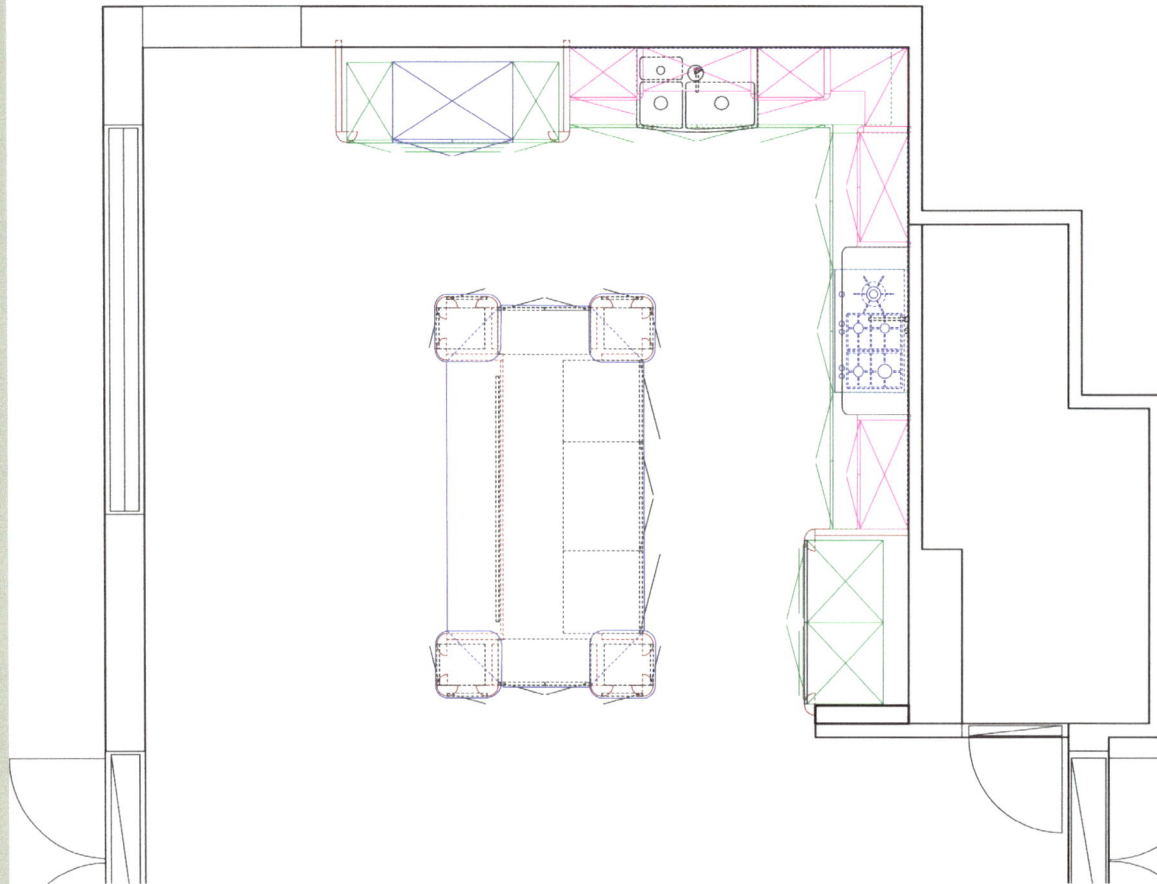

Sail
Natural
Grain Painted

Natural
Hamilton Oak
Cabinets

Special
Natural
Grain Painted

Abstract
Expressions
Natural
Halifax Oak

Grey Tint
Mirror

**Netherton
Natural
Grain Painted**

**Natural
Carini Walnut
Cabinets**

**Orphic
Expressions
Dark Baysen
Oak**

**Orphic
Tigerwood
Nero**

Perfect Situation
Alternative 2
Project 020

Inspiration

PUSHING BOUNDARIES:
Invitation to Pandora's Box & a Multitude of Possibilities

Volte face: A complete reversal of position in argument or opinion. The English Dictionary definition says it all - whether in relation to the two prior designs for this kitchen or the eclectic and colourful nature of the materials and finishes. This a perfect example on which to conclude this section – as it epitomises why engaging a design-led kitchen specialist can open up unimaginable opportunities.

DESIGN DYNAMICS

The Art of Crafting Kitchen Showroom Displays

Celebrating four decades in design, innovation meets inspiration as showrooms tell a tale of passion and precision.

021
Industrial Grace

022
Tranquil Dining

023
Urban Allure

An aspect of 40+ years of involvement in the design and manufacture of kitchens which truly stands out for me has been the privilege to engage in the design and creation of innovative kitchen displays in association with Callerton colleagues and our National Network of Kitchen Specialist Retailers.

A privilege, a passion & a testament to design's transformative power

As explained in my intro to 'Insights' - kitchen design is my equivalent to Crosswords, Sudoku and Wordle. I find it fascinating, an intellectual challenge and one I relish – creating designs involving the latest concepts and ideas to wow those in the market for a new kitchen provides a buzz. Design is in my blood and the creation of a successful showroom an aspect of my role I've much enjoyed.

I should point out there is a distinction between creating an individual display and developing a successful showroom involving multiple displays. An excellent demonstration as to what's entailed relates to a project produced during the 'Covid-19 Pandemic' when showrooms were closed by Government decree. To answer this we created the 'Virtual Studio' as demonstrated by the imagery.

To gain a better insight to this project log onto www.rk-tec.co.uk and the 'Virtual Studio'.

The aim of any display is to demonstrate the three vital ingredients required of all successful kitchens: - Great design, great products and great project management - plus inspiring clients and broadening their horizons. To demonstrate this we've picked out a diverse array of ten thought provoking displays from Callerton's National Network of Design-led Kitchen Specialist Retailers.

024
Eclectic Luxe

A successful showroom captures the essence of great design, impeccable products & meticulous project management, together inspiring a vision

025
Graceful
Opulence

026
Sophisticated
Form

027
Sublime
Oasis

028
Modern
Majesty

029
Timeless
Grandeur

030
Refined
Luxury

Industrial Grace
Display
Project 021

UNIFIED VISION:
A Collaborative Design Journey for Contemporary Kitchen Brilliance

In most instances the process involved in creating a kitchen project includes the client, or clients and their chosen design specialist. Not in this instance where the whole combined Design-led Retailer Team interacted with Callerton's display department to produce a stand-out scheme. Contemporary clean cut lines with high gloss furniture and contrasting timber elements proves to be highly effective.

Tranquil Dining Display

Project 022

DIMINUTIVE DESIGN:
Mastery of Space
in a Petite Oasis

An object lesson and demonstration as what can be achieved when confronted with constrained dimensions. Form, function and style come to the fore in the layout of this delightful kitchen. The peninsular design enables dedicated wet, hob and preparation areas – plus a breakfast bar. The tall floating bank encapsulates ovens, fridge/freezer and storage – a master class in diminutive design.

Urban Allure
Display
Project 023

MULTITUDE OF MACHINATIONS:
Crafting Harmony in this Metropolitan Kitchen Display

Balance, symmetry and detail come to the fore in this stylish city centre display kitchen. A design encompassing much: - TV cabinetry and formal dining, intertwined with a relaxed breakfast bar incorporated into an island with stand-out features and practicality. The hob and sink, plus copious preparation capacity is overlooked by a floating tall appliance bank with intriguing open cabinetry.

Eclectic Luxe
Display
Project 024

CROSSOVER/HYBRID:
A Fusion of High Tech
& Shaker Elegance

A fine example of crossover/hybrid design incorporating high tech contemporary elements with Shaker and so much more. Modern industrial materials meld exceptionally well with traditional painted furniture. But so much more is contained within this outstanding example: - Built-in curved bench seating, sleek modern canopy, lounge furniture and TV area – a thought provoking illustration.

Graceful Opulence
Display
Project 025

DRAMATIC STATEMENT:
A Kitchen Where Style & Functionality Meet

A kitchen with plenty of panache and flamboyance. The combination of the striking island, tall bank and wet area - a consummate lesson in relation to the fundamental elements of form and function. The island with curved breakfast bar and open cabinetry, the tall bank incorporating a butler's pantry along with glazed and open elements, the Belfast sink and dishwashing area and detail – spectacular.

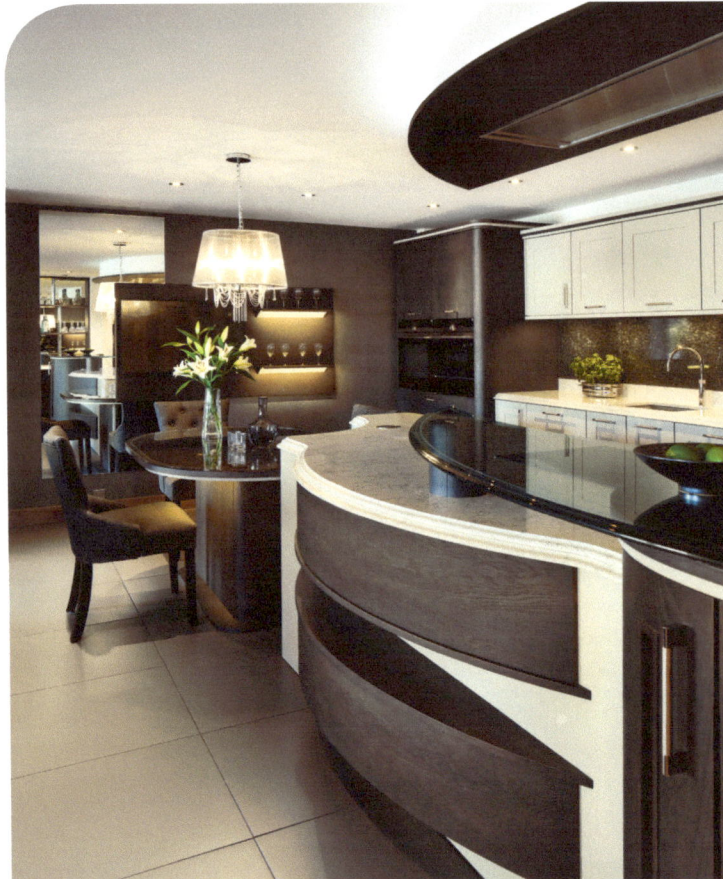

Sophisticated Form
Display
Project 026

CURVACEOUS CREATION:
The Art of Sinuous Design in a Crossover/ Hybrid Kitchen

Curves come to the fore in this spectacular Crossover/Hybrid kitchen along with a mix of stained flat panelled Oak and Shaker painted cabinetry. The island with its curvaceous form emphasised via the double wing, glazed pillar box, tear-drop breakfast bar, plus integrated table and leg. The tall bank no less impressive – radiused features seamlessly integrate the imposing refrigeration and cabinetry.

Sublime Oasis
Display
Project 027

BRAVADO & INDIVIDUALITY:
Crafting a Unique Kitchen with Contemporary Flair & Classic Accents

Traditional and contemporary elements combine to create a kitchen for the discerning client looking for something that bit different. Matt contemporary elements along with oak veneers, plus radiused features - add a touch of brass and Shaker painted finishes, gives you something truly individual. Also of note the unusual shape of island design incorporating the table and bench seating – exquisite.

Modern Majesty
Display
Project 028

CLASSIC CONTEMPORARY COMBO:
Blending High Tech Functionality with Shaker Sophistication

A modern high tech and Shaker combination highlights the ability to create something different and timeless. The contemporary matt furniture alongside Shaker painted cabinetry interspersed with the light oak open-shelving and breakfast bar elements, plus the contrasting colours of the worksurfaces - makes for a bold statement. The practicality and functionality of the design also deserves mention.

Timeless Grandeur
Display

SYMMETRY & STYLE:
A Harmonious Design Embraces Form, Function & Elegant Symmetry

Form, function, balance, symmetry and style combine effortlessly in this Shaker inspired kitchen. The ceiling height allows for an imposing chimney breast and mantle with corresponding tall wall cabinetry incorporating glazed top-box elements. A variety of attributes stand-out: - Open shelving, pillar box, butler's pantry, tall bank, radiused-island with circular breakfast bar – plus so much more.

Refined Luxury
Display
Project 030

INTEGRATED ELEGANCE:
A Bold Statement Derived via Innovative Features & Striking Detail

A copious amount of signature and feature items integrated into this elegant kitchen stamp their mark and make a bold statement: - The impressive chimney canopy, unusual concave island open shelving, the glass table and dramatic base, innovative and striking TV detail, the glazed pillar box cabinet with integrated chopping block, plus worksurface and backsplash detail - to name just a few.

RK-Tec

Celebrating 15 Years of Kitchen Excellence, Collaboration & Design Innovation

LEGACY

**RK-Tec Legacy:
Celebrating 15 Years of Kitchen
Excellence, Collaboration,
and Design Innovation**

The RK-Tec (revolutionary kitchen techniques) initiative involves ten leading brand names from the kitchen industry. Whose aim is to promote the three vital ingredients required of all successful kitchen projects: - Great Design, Great Products and Great Project Management. As examined and highlighted by the various and varied projects incorporated within 'Insights to Kitchen Design'.

RK-Tec came about at the time of the '2008 Financial Crash' and aimed to be an antidote to the doom and gloom surrounding that period. The RK-Tec partners recognising the combination of all the many products incorporated into a 'Dream Kitchen' are more powerful than the individual items. They also engaged in providing education and training when going about creating such projects.

As someone actively involved with the RK-Tec initiative from its early days - I wanted to recognise the farsighted companies and individuals who agreed to engage in the project. Fifteen years on RK-Tec continue to produce an annual publication 'Kitchen Inspiration' to promote the importance of 'Great Design, Great Products & Great Project Management' - as well as their various training programmes.

'Insights to Kitchen Design' incorporates a plethora of kitchens utilising products from RK-Tec members and without their input and involvement this book may well have not come about. Hence my reasoning as to including a final section highlighting the RK-Tec partners and their innovative products. 'Insights' aim has been to demonstrate successful projects involve a wide range of facets.

This section seeks to highlight the diversity of these and an opportunity to say 'Thank You'.

Hence my decision the final aspect of 'Insights' should revolve around a series of interviews with senior luminaries from the RK-Tec initiative - to extract pearls of wisdom as to their brands, as well as demonstrating a smidgen, as to the multitude of diverse products involved in design-led kitchens.

031

032

The RK-Tec initiative involves ten leading brand names from the kitchen industry, aiming to promote the three vital ingredients required of all successful kitchen projects: Great Design, Great Products, & Great Project Management

036

037

038

033

034

SIEMENS

035

039

Invented for life

040

Callerton
Turning Dreams to Reality

The final aspect of 'Insights' revolves around a series of interviews with senior luminaries from the RK-Tec initiative

031 - HINGES, DRAWERS, INTERNAL MANAGEMENT & MORE

40+ years in the Design-led Kitchen Specialist World highlights the vital aspects required of all successful projects, plus one other often overlooked. To assemble the multitude of diverse elements and components (every one of equal importance to ensure a dream kitchen turns to reality) relies on that further critical ingredient - being mutually beneficial partnerships and long-term relationships.

The following pages attempt to highlight examples of such: -

As a manufacturer Callerton are totally reliant on the availability of all raw materials and components being attainable at the required time and of the necessary quality to ensure the furniture element of a kitchen achieves the requested timescale. Blum have been our default supplier of drawers, hinges and so much more for over 30+ years – a vital aspect of our business.

To highlight the relationship I spoke with David Sanders (Blum's Sales and Marketing Director) whom I've known for a great many years. The focus of my questioning revolved around understanding what Blum's brand stands for and its philosophy. David's answer was revealing: -

'Moving ideas' lies at the heart of our brand, a dynamic philosophy built upon seven core values (Quality, Innovation, Inspiration, Quality of Living, Product Range, Trust, and Services). Each of these values serves as a guiding principle, shaping the essence of our brand and the way we interact with the world.

Together, these seven core values constitute the basis of moving ideas, propelling our brand forward and shaping a purpose-driven narrative that goes beyond the products we offer. It's not just about what we create; it's about the values we uphold and the impact we aim to make on the world.

Our brand is built on a foundation of trust, driven by forward-thinking solutions and an unyielding dedication to adapting to the dynamic needs of our customers. Our brand identity is intricately woven into the fabric of our commitment to excellence, symbolising not just a promise, but a relentless pursuit of unparalleled quality and innovation.

We strive to create a single high-level brand experience by providing quality products, exceptional customer service, and a dedication to ongoing innovation. We are committed to these values and to upholding them in every interaction we have with our customers. We stay in motion to move ideas forward.

I can personally vouch for this having worked in partnership with Blum for 30+ years – and leave the imagery to highlight and provide an insight into their amazing and innovative product range. One final statement from David highlights Blum's underlying values and confidence in their products: -

Blum's unique selling proposition is anchored in its unwavering commitment to innovation, quality, and user-centric design, underscored by a lifetime guarantee on their products.

David Sanders explains Blum's ethos: "'Moving ideas' lies at the heart of our brand, a dynamic philosophy built upon seven core values: Quality, Innovation, Inspiration, Quality of Living, Product Range, Trust, & Services."

↑blum®

032 - APPLIANCES: COOKING PASSION SINCE 1877

The development in relation to appliances since I entered the Design-led Kitchen Specialist World (40+ Years ago) has been stratospheric.

The technology, functionality and sophistication could well have come from outer-space compared to what was available to us all those years ago. I could never have envisaged the advances and the multifaceted nature of all that is now on the market.

Callerton's relationship with NEFF goes back to our very early days. Names from the past such as Uwe Hanneck and Mike Jarrett will be recognisable to those of a certain age and demonstrate the long-term nature of our partnership. The baton has since been passed on and I've worked closely with the next generation for a considerable number of years - one such person being Simon Jones.

My relationship and friendship with Simon goes back a number of years and his title 'Director, Kitchen Division' relates to the BSH Group which encompasses the NEFF, Siemens & Bosch brands. So what better person to provide an insight to the World of appliances. Hence I've utilised his words alongside a series of images to highlight what is now available to the discerning client.

His opening line being: - *At NEFF we believe that the kitchen is the heart of every home. A place to eat, meet and get creative with your cooking. With an extensive range of innovative appliances, we're constantly working to meet the demands of every lifestyle.*

From there we moved onto examining a series of NEFF products to better understand the wide and varied nature of their extensive range and an insight to the many advances involved with these.

SLIDE & HIDE® – THE ONLY OVEN WITH A DISAPPEARING DOOR

Slide & Hide® is simply the first choice for individualists, who want to enjoy their passion for cooking without limitations. Our iconic Slide & Hide® door effortlessly slides away beneath the oven when not in use. So nothing gets in the way of your creativity. Get up close and personal to season and stir your favourite dishes.

CIRCO THERM® – HOT AIR SYSTEM FOR SIMULTANEOUS COOKING

Circo Therm® hot air technology focusses heat directly on the food being cooked, so surfaces of bakes and roasts are sealed quickly. This seals in moisture makes meats juicier and cakes delicious and moist.

INTENSIVE STEAM

Intensify flavours and preserve nutrients Experience Full Steam with the new Intensive Steam feature with 120°C heat that retains your ingredient's nutrients and taste, for deliciously moist and flavoursome results.

+ NEFF NEW TWIST PAD®

INCREASE YOUR FLEXIBILITY & SPACE IN COOLING

Having extra room can really open you up a world of possibilities. With the latest 289 litre XL and 381 litre XXL fridge-freezer combinations, you'll have ample space to accommodate your biggest culinary dreams. Imagine being able to effortlessly store entire trays of baked goods or sizable watermelons without having to rearrange everything else in the fridge. That large additional space is like a secret ingredient that can take your cooking to the next level and invite even more deliciousness into your life.

NEW TWIST PAD®

On selected models there is a brand new Twist Pad®. Using the same control to point and twist to operate the hob, this also features a graphite grey trim to accessorize to the oven trim.*This new Twist Pad® is available on selected N90 Flex induction hobs.*

FRYING SENSOR

The sensor automatically adjusts the heat to the pan to maintain an even temperature. This control allows you to cook all dishes to perfection as it maintains a consistent heat preventing overcooking or burning.

HOB HOOD CONTROL

Being able to control the hood directly from the hob means the hood turns on when you start cooking and, in automatic mode, can automatically regulate the power level for the best performance with the lowest noise – it also means you no longer need to worry about adjusting the hood and you can focus on your cooking.

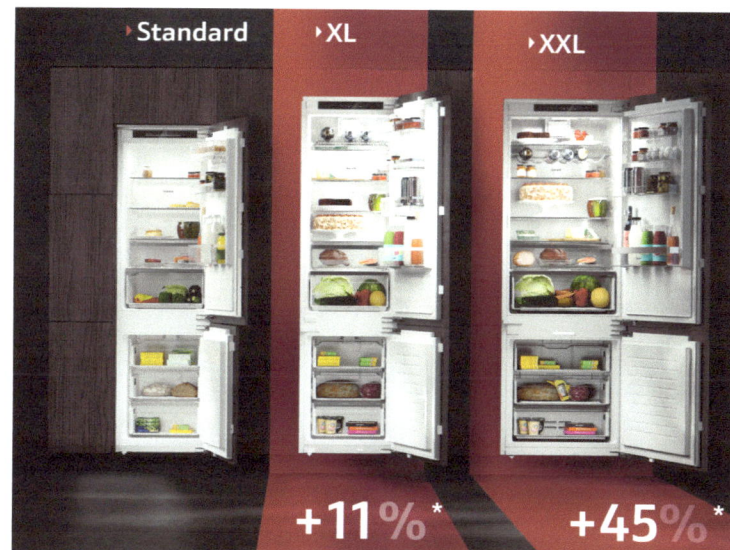

Standard   XL   XXL

+11%*   +45%*

+ LATEST NEFF FRIDGE FREEZER COMBINATIONS

+ NEFF SLIDE & HIDE®

NEFF
cook. create. inspire.

A vital element of any kitchen relates to the supply of fresh water and disposal of waste: - Hence sinks, taps (filtered, boiling, etc), as well as waste management systems are important aspects of all successful projects. A kitchen without these essentials - would cease to function.

The RK-Tec initiative aims to highlight the plethora of diverse ingredients required to produce a design-led kitchen. Sinks, taps and waste management are important entities and developments in this particular area over my 40+ years in the Industry have been vast – the following imagery is designed to accentuate various aspects of such.

To expand on their speciality I spoke with Neil Clark (Cluster Head Northern Europe & Sub-Saharan Africa) whom I've known for 20+ years - our relationship with Franke going back even further. Being World leaders in their field I wanted Neil to enlighten us on Franke's brand values and ethos. Here he provides an insight: -

Founded in 1911 in Switzerland, Franke epitomises a century-long commitment to pushing the boundaries of innovation and product excellence. As the world's leading sink manufacturer, Franke has evolved into a comprehensive system provider known for seamlessly integrating exclusive design with full functionality, Swiss quality, and sustainable innovations for a better life.

Franke Home Solutions, a division of the Franke Group, is a world-leading provider of intelligent systems and solutions for the residential kitchen. The brand's philosophy revolves around a holistic system approach, offering an impeccable range of kitchen products, including sinks, taps, waste management solutions, and appliances all distinguished by industry-leading and award-winning designs.

Globally renowned, Franke is celebrated for its extensive product range and a strategic commitment to ensuring that its products are not only aesthetically beautiful but also practical and functional. The brand envisions intuitive home solutions that bring joy to everyday use, combining precision engineering with traditional craftsmanship. Franke's commitment to excellence is evident in its exclusive use of the finest materials, colours, finishes, and textures, resulting in elegant and ergonomic products that stand the test of time, while reflecting and anticipating the evolving tastes and preferences of today's discerning consumers.

+ VITAL CAPSULE FILTER 3-IN-1 J-SPOUT TAP IN MATT BLACK / DECOR STEEL PVD

Insight's to Kitchen Design celebrates the ability of the design-led kitchen specialist to create spectacular kitchens that perform all the many diverse needs and requirements for each individual client. Franke provides what are essential elements (sinks, taps & waste management) and as per all the many other ingredients involved - there is so much more to this area than people give credit.

Neil Clark of Franke UK provides insights into the brand:

"Founded in 1911 in Switzerland, Franke epitomises a century-long commitment to innovation & product excellence."

+ MYTHOS MASTERPIECE BXM 210/110-68 IN COPPER, WITH ATLAS NEO SWIVEL SPOUT TAP AND ATLAS NEO SOAP DISPENSER IN COPPER

FRANKE

034 - APPLIANCES: PROGRESS THROUGH CURIOSITY

A continuation of my conversation with Simon Jones (Director, Kitchen Division for the BSH Group) in relation to the Siemens brand and their innovative range of products. He proffered the following insight as to this and then highlighted the broad range of areas they are engaged with: -

When outstanding engineering, break-through technology and head-turning design is innovatively combined, the result is Siemens. The brilliant innovations found in Siemens Home Appliances, not only set a new standard in applied technology, they redefine the way we run our households. For the past 100 years, the brand Siemens stands for breakthrough technologies, engineered to revolutionise the home.

With more than 350 international design awards in the past ten years, it is abundantly clear that Siemens has found a winning recipe.

In an age where home appliances need to meet the on-the-go lifestyle of its consumers, Siemens is one step ahead. Offering products that not only lead the way in smart technology and unparalleled user experiences, but in lasting, clear design aesthetics too.

Simon was keen to explain the importance of sustainability and what this means for Siemens: -

We are convinced that an environmentally friendly lifestyle does not require compromising on comfort or performance. To preserve our natural resources, we engage in developing sustainable innovations together with long-lasting design. We aim to minimise the environmental impact of our products from production to usage, so that you can enjoy using Siemens Home Appliances in a sustainable way.

Simon's explanation as to the depth of the Siemens product range: -

+ ADVANCED SIEMENS TECHNOLOGY & INTELLIGENT FEATURES

OVENS

Siemens built-in ovens boast a stylish design and offer flexibility in installation, allowing them to fit under work surfaces, in tall units, or alongside other appliances. This flexibility enhances kitchen design options. These ovens also feature advanced technology and intelligent features that save time during cooking.

COMPACTS

With the variety of appliances in our compact built-in range, Siemens provides a combination of options to suit your preferences, while delivering complete visual perfection. Siemens 45cm and 38cm high compact appliances allow for a full array of cooking configurations. Depending on the range and model, compact ovens are available with steam or integrated microwave, offering space-saving design without compromising on style or utility.

+ THE NEW SIEMENS GLASSDRAFTAIR

+ SIEMENS LC91KLT60 COOKER HOOD & EX975LXC1E INDUCTION HOB

HOBS

With intelligent technology, elegant design aesthetics and practical yet impressive functionality, Siemens hobs bring excitement and ease when creating dishes. Siemens aim to provide a wide selection of quality hob choices to ensure there is enough variety and colour-ways to choose from to match your kitchen style. From stunning indctionAir plus hobs to a classic gas hob, there's a premium Siemens hob to consider for any kitchen.

HOODS

Outstanding performance, intelligently designed. Whether you choose a sleek ceiling hood, state-of-the-art glassdraftAir hood, a stylish chimney hood or integrated style hood our solutions will provide innovative design and a stylish finish to your kitchen. Selected Siemens hoods come with a quiet and energy efficient motor so you can cook in a more comfortable surrounding.

DISHWASHERS

Siemens built-in dishwashers offer a modern design and innovative features to enhance the user experience. Key innovations include varioSpeed Plus, which speeds up washing programs by 30% to 70%, and Zeolith® drying technology for efficient and gentle drying. These dishwashers also have height-adjustable baskets, foldable racks, and stylish features like door openAssist, sideLight, and timeLight floor projection. These elements combine to offer a balance of modern design and advanced technology.

REFRIGERATION

Siemens offers a range of built-in refrigeration appliances, including fridges, freezers, and wine coolers, designed for flexible storage and optimal freshness of food. These appliances come in various sizes and models, allowing for customised combinations to meet individual needs, tastes, and kitchen designs. Each Siemens cooling appliance enhances convenience and freshness, providing flexibility in kitchen planning.

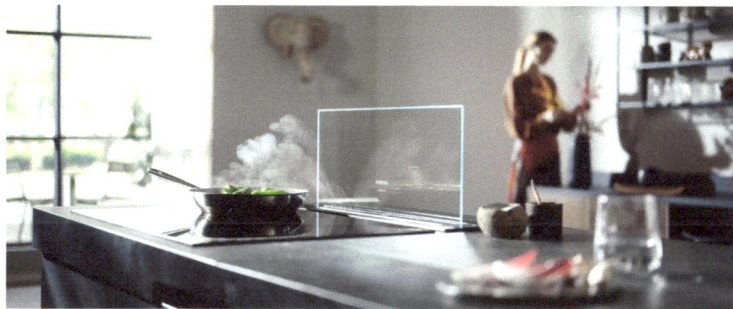

+ SIEMENS A-COOL

LAUNDRY

Laundry care, high performance with state-of-the-art technology. Siemens has created a built-in laundry range that is cleverly designed and quietly efficient, developed to make laundry easier and less of a chore.

SIEMENS

Callerton's relationship with Cosentino and their various brands pertains to their involvement with the RK-Tec initiative and their innovative products being incorporated into several of the houses at Potton's Show Centre (St Neots) - as featured in earlier 'Insights' kitchen case-studies. It would be remiss not to point out Cosentino have worked with Callerton's National Network of Design-led Kitchen Specialists for many decades – so by default our relationship goes back much further.

At a recent meeting with members of the Cosentino Team in relation to compiling detail to produce this piece about them and their products – I was blown away by the company's story, as well as the range of diverse applications they are engaged with. Hence – Worksurfaces & So Much More.

The following is a brief extract as to what I learnt from our session: -

Cosentino Group is a global family-owned company that produces and distributes high value innovative and sustainable surfaces for architecture and design. As a leading company, Cosentino imagines and anticipates together with its customers and partners design solutions that offer value and inspiration to people's lives. This goal is made possible by pioneering brands that are leaders in their respective segments such as Silestone®, Dekton® and Sensa by Cosentino®.

The group bases its development on international expansion, an innovative research and development program, respect for the environment and sustainability, and its ongoing corporate commitment to society and the local communities where it operates, education, equality and health & safety.

Cosentino Group currently distributes its products and brands in more than 120 countries, from its headquarters in Almeria (Spain), and it's present with its own assets in 31 of them. The group has 9 factories (8 in Almería, Spain and 1 in Brazil), 1 intelligent logistic platform in Spain, and 140 commercial and business units throughout the world. More than 90% of Cosentino Group's financial turnover comes from international markets.

+ SILESTONE URBAN CRUSH

+ SILESTONE ECLECTIC PEARL

Parisian Blue - Taking inspiration from the French Capital. This colourway boasts a deep bluish tone with strong personality and powerful character. Inspired by the shades seen in famous Imperial Roman stones, combined with fine veins in ochre tones.

Victorian Silver - Soft and subtle two-toned marbling in the background, with gradient effects and depth. The cool background tone blends with its silver and dark grey veins to create an elegant colour that fits seamlessly with warm and cold tones.

Eclectic Pearl - One of the best examples of the core design idea behind Le Chic. Classic and modern, it features flowing streams of delicate tones incrusted with grains like diamonds on jewelry. Eclectic Pearl hypnotises with delicate veining, texture, and metallic accents across the whole surface.

Bohemian Flame - This colour presents subtle sinuous veins with metallic inlays in copper shades. The movement of the golden flows of lava that generate scars on volcanic soil inspires it. It's reminiscent of the calmly moving golden flame of candles accentuating tiny metallic pieces.

Versailles Ivory - The warmest tone of the collection. Very subtle two-toned marbling in the background with gradient effects mesmerise with the flickering lights of its golden sparkle. Versailles Ivory exudes luxury and elegance, reminiscent of the exuberance of the Palace of Versailles.

Romantic Ash - Another example of Le Chic's visual excellence. Large rivers and incrustations of grains in various sizes awaken memories of a milky way visible on a clear starry sky. The accent of blue strengthens the depth of Romantic Ash.

I cannot do the story in relation to the development of their company justice in the space available, suffice to say it is worth looking into this – mightily impressive. In relation to their extensive and innovative product range I picked out one of their most recent – Le Chic: -

Cosentino has launched Le Chic, the latest product offering from Silestone®. A juxtaposition to the more modern look of the Urban Crush series, Le Chic brings elegance and sophistication to the home.

This new Silestone® series redefines a timeless classic. A step forward in veined-patterned surfacing with six designs available, that take inspiration from Victorian and Parisian spaces, with a nod to nostalgia with a modern execution. Le Chic collection is an elegant and sophisticated offering that can be used in all areas in the house. The patterns feature expressive veins and metallic accents that stand out against neutral backdrops like cream or deep blues and blacks, creating depth.

Le Chic collection is composed of six designs: Parisian Blue, Eclectic Pearl, Versailles Ivory, Victorian Silver, Bohemian Flame and Romantic Ash.

silestone®

Designed by COSENTINO

036 - COMPUTER AIDED DESIGN & SPECIFICATION

I don't believe I need to explain more or demonstrate the critical importance of CAD (Computer Aided Design) in the creation of a design inspired kitchen project: The 20 actual projects, along with the 40 alternative designs featured in 'Insights', testify to the value and significance of this vital tool.

The aspect of our relationship with Cyncly and the relevance of the partnership not only for Callerton and all involved in our National Network of Design-led Kitchen Specialist Retailers requires further explanation. This is a critical element and aspect for all as not only does the software enable and provide 3D CAD drawings – but also codes, costs, specifies, and orders the kitchen.

Hence rather than show more 3D CAD imagery we've utilised a project to demonstrate the broader ability in relation to all that is made available in the background via Winner, Cyncly's software. Before so doing I will utilise elements of a discussion with Alex Ainge, Senior Director – Head of KBF Retail Sales (SMB & Mid-Market) – EMEA at Cyncly, as to their brand values, ethos and aspirations – which provides an interesting insight to their craft and proposition.

Cyncly's end-to-end software solutions connect designers, retailers, manufacturers, contractors and consumers to make spaces amazing. We are creating a future where spaces for living are designed, built and sold to inspire, more sustainably and efficiently.

From project start to finish – from inspiration to installation – whether the project entails a new build or a renovation, Cyncly equips companies in the spaces-for-living industry with software solutions that create a seamless connection between design inspiration and realisation. Businesses use our software to transform vision into reality with speed, flexibility, and efficiency.

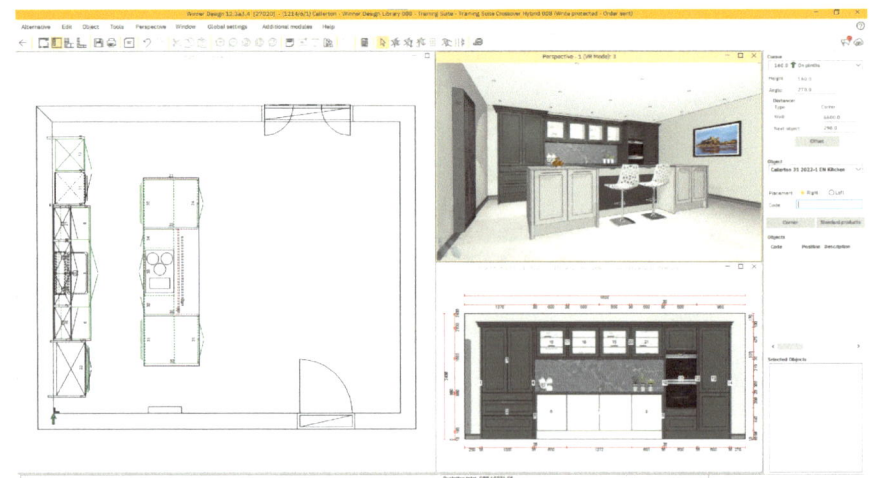

+ WINNER FLEX SCREENSHOT

Alex Ainge of Cyncly discusses their brand values:

"Cyncly's end-to-end software solutions connect designers, retailers, manufacturers, contractors, & consumers to make spaces amazing."

With the world's largest repository of catalogues and solutions for every step of the process, including CAD design applications, CPQ solutions, business process management, manufacturing execution systems and enterprise resource planning, Cyncly offers a connected platform that enables a seamless flow of information across the business. Companies use our software as a way to build their business: to scale up, diversify their offerings, and manufacture with greater flexibility and efficiency.

Hopefully, this provides an appreciation as to the relevance of our relationship and the critical nature the software provides to our company. The partnership and effort required from both parties (Callerton & Cyncly) being in a position to design, code, specify, cost and order a kitchen, as well as providing all the working drawings and information to project manage such should not be underestimated.

Callerton's involvement with Cyncly goes back some 20+ years and I hope 'Insights' helps to demonstrate the significance and value this brings to our Design-led Kitchen Specialist Retailers, ourselves, and most important of all the end client. A critical aspect of turning 'Dreams to Reality'.

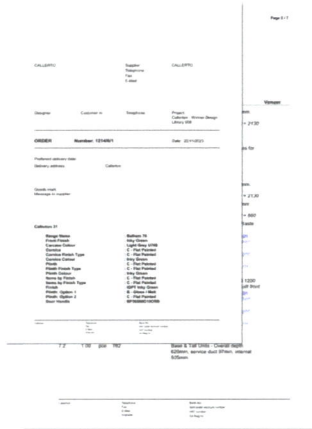

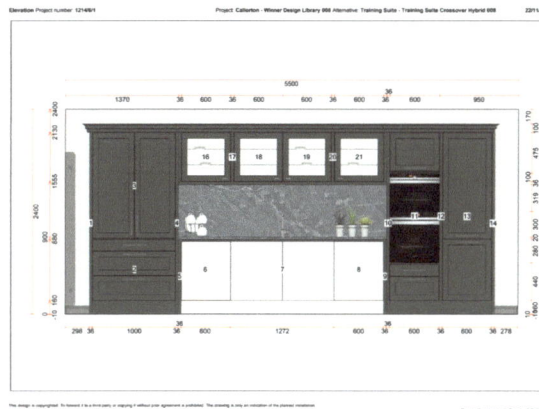

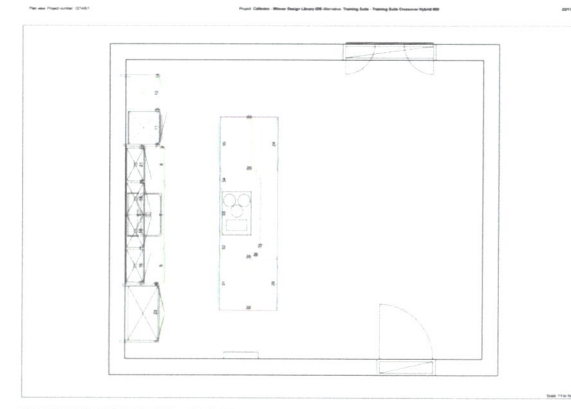

+ ORDER PRODUCED FROM WINNER FLEX

+ RENDER FROM WINNER FLEX

Cyncly

037 - WORKSURFACES & SO MUCH MORE

In the prior Silestone pages I introduced Cosentino -

the organisation behind these exceptional products. Those with an eagle eye may have noticed a reference to Dekton which deserves additional explanation – this a further Cosentino brand and an interesting product. From my session with their Team I learnt not only its attributes - but also the wide range of applications.

+ DEKTON TK06 MAROMORIO

+ DEKTON GK07 CEPPO AND VK02 AVORIO

The following aims to provide an insight to these – just some of what I learnt from our session: -

Dekton® by Cosentino is a revolutionary and innovative Ultracompact stone for architecture and design. It is a sophisticated mixture of minerals and a unique ultra-compaction press process. Its set of superior technical properties, such as resistance to UV rays, scratches, stains and thermal shock and very low water absorption, make Dekton® the perfect surface for a wide range of applications, both indoors and outdoors. In 2020, Dekton® earned the Carbon Neutral product certification for its entire colour portfolio, standing out as the only cradle-to-grave carbon-neutral surface.

I found it fascinating that Dekton is so much more than a kitchen worksurface and has multiple uses not only within the home – but also in commercial situations. As someone from the kitchen specialist world I was aware of Dekton in relation to worksurfaces, upstands, back splashes and panelling within a kitchen environment. Before moving on I thought it worth pointing out Callerton's Product Development Team are working on and prototyping the usage of such within cabinetry and frontals.

Dekton is an incredibly versatile product and here we demonstrate further applications: -

Dekton, by global leader Cosentino, leads the way when it comes to offering best-in-class hotel surfaces. The revolutionary, ultra-compact stone is a sophisticated mixture of raw minerals made with Sinterized Particle Technology (TSP) and a unique compaction press process which eliminates micro-defects that cause tension or weak points, giving its surfaces superior properties that are exceptional for hospitality spaces. From exterior facades and cladding, to interior staircases, furniture, worktops and bathrooms, with Dekton multi-application specifications can all be done from one place.

Its long-term resistance to UV rays, abrasion, stains, extreme heat or cold and its low water absorption make it the perfect surface to withstand the demanding needs of a hotel.

Whether in areas such as restaurants and bars that must withstand regular, acidic spillages and scratches, or high-traffic spaces like lobbies and staircases that must be ultra hard-wearing and durable, hotel surfaces must be able to keep pace. With Dekton, they can.

Its unique properties that enable these benefits, also make Dekton surfaces easy to clean. Natural stones such as marble require far more maintenance and care – becoming easily slippery and prone to damage. As Dekton is a technological material, it is ideal for spaces like bathrooms which are exposed to moisture and where regular cleaning is essential. Its non-porous surface discourages the growth of bacteria and mould, making it the more hygienic choice.

Dekton also offers more design freedom. Its impressive range of larger slab sizes eliminates the need for multiple join lines helping create more seamless aesthetics. An extensive range of slab thicknesses allows for increased flexibility for designers, alongside Dekton's impressive colour ranges in its existing product portfolio. For a fully bespoke offering, Dekton ID enables ultimate customisation for any space.

As a carbon neutral material throughout its entire lifecycle, Dekton's ability to be used within more sustainable construction is particularly significant.

+ DEKTON VK03 GRIGIO

DEKTON®

Designed by COSENTINO

038 - FURNITURE LIGHTING SOLUTIONS

Lighting is a critical ingredient of all design-led kitchens – renege or cut back on this aspect of a project will inevitably prove detrimental and diminish the finished article. This relates not only to performance and function, but also looks and ambience.

+ SENSIO HYPE TRIOTONE® TECHNOLOGY ALLOWS YOU TO SELECT WARM, NATURAL, OR COOL WHITE

No need to take my word for this – peruse the imagery of the 20 kitchen case-studies featured within Insights. Then imagine each of these with all lighting excluded or turned off.

The individual items involved in the creation of a kitchen stand for little when compared to the finished article incorporating all the many diverse elements and their amalgamation. Lighting is a critical piece in the jigsaw and to learn more I spoke with Michael Linsky (MD of Sensio).

Here a brief insight to lighting from an expert in his field: -

Lighting can completely transform your space beyond the practical benefits it brings. It creates ambience, a brighter more spacious and multi-dimensional feel, and highlights features. Considering a lighting scheme at the initial stages will influence the overall atmosphere of an interior space.

The areas we illuminate in our kitchen can be categorised into three key sections, each of these three key lighting sections should be carefully considered throughout your design process, paying attention to features you wish to illuminate as well as how you will practically interact with your new space.

Task Lighting – perfectly positioned to ensure your kitchen is an efficient space for everyday tasks such as cooking. Typically, kitchen task lighting is positioned under wall cabinetry to illuminate the work-surface, focusing lighting exactly where it is needed.

Convenience Lighting – illuminates doored cabinetry and drawers when opened for ultimate ease of use, while adding a luxurious finish to the design. Say goodbye to dark spots and say hello to fully useable and beautiful storage solutions.

Mood lighting creates depth and dimension which is essential for creating atmosphere within a room. Mood lighting is often overlooked, but one that can have a profound impact. Consider floor-level recessed lighting, up-lighting above wall cabinetry, lighting beneath breakfast bars or the underside of a work-surface, integrated lighting within open and glazed features.

Ensure your new interior space provides the perfect atmosphere for everyday life and entertainment.

Wise words making the point lighting is not an add-on but requires to be at the forefront when creating a dream kitchen. Callerton's partnership with Sensio emphasises the importance of working together – many lighting solutions involve integration within the furniture. Hence lighting and furniture manufacturer require to work in step with one another. I leave the final word to Michael: -

Design and innovation are at the core of Sensio, striving for simplicity without compromise. Since 2007 we've been creating lighting in harmony with modern life. Quality and innovation has always been at the heart of what we do, from lighting that stands the test of time to technology that's exclusive to us - and working alongside enlighted furniture manufacturers such as Callerton.

Michael Linsky of Sensio explains: "Lighting can completely transform your space beyond the practical benefits it brings. It creates ambience, a brighter more spacious & multi-dimensional feel, & highlights features."

sensio®
furniture lighting solutions

039 - APPLIANCES: BOSCH INVENTED FOR LIFE

My marathon session with Simon Jones (Director Kitchen Division at BSH Group) culminated in looking into and gaining an understanding as to their Bosch brand and range of appliances. As previously explained we have worked with all three brands over many years – aptly demonstrated by our joint involvement with Potton's show centre as featured in four 'Insights to Kitchen Design' projects.

Simon began his explanation of Bosch by asking a question 'Who Are Bosch?' – with an enlightening answer: -

'I'd rather lose money than trust' – Robert Bosch, 1921. For over 130 years, the Bosch name has been synonymous with engineering excellence. Our home appliances are renowned for their quality, reliability and performance which derives from an inherent, unflagging commitment and thoroughness with which every unit is made.

As you would expect from Bosch, there are no gimmicks or frills with our products – just pure, clean lines and beautiful, functional simplicity that will enhance any kitchen.

Once more Simon was keen to explain their attitude and approach to sustainability: -

At Bosch we provide innovative and efficient solutions helping you save energy, water and reduce food waste. Durability is key when focusing on sustainability, which is why Bosch products are designed and built to last. At Bosch, we've been creating home appliances for 90 years and ensure that all our products are designed and tested to perform consistently throughout their lifetime. We know how much reliability and peace of mind matters.

Simon followed this with a brief outline and insight as to what Bosch's product range entails: -

Whatever kind of cook you are, we have a range of smart and stylish built-in single or double ovens for you to choose from. Serve up vitamin-packed meals using one of our innovative added steam ovens or, if limited on space, our easy-to-use microwaves and compact appliances will bring style and function to any kitchen.

Bosch fridges and freezers use energy-efficient technologies and innovative systems such as VitaFresh and No Frost for effective cooling and freezing, helping you live a more sustainable lifestyle.

+ BOSCH PVQ811F15E SERIES 6 INDUCTION HOB WITH INTEGRATED VENTILATION SYSTEM

Bosch hobs are packed with innovative technology that's designed to make cooking more intuitive. A choice of gas, ceramic and induction hobs gives you the flexibility to cook how you want and contemporary design makes the most of your kitchen.

Our cooker hoods effectively remove cooking odours and capture grease from the air. High performance, low noise, and available in the look you want, find your perfect helper for a clean-looking, fresh-smelling kitchen.

+ BOSCH DWK85DK60 INCLINED HOOD

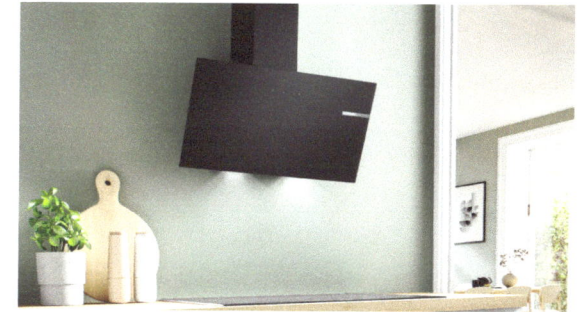

+ PERFECTDRY DISHWASHERS WITH ZEOLITH TECHNOLOGY

Our cleverly designed range of dishwashers makes dishes, glassware and more come out spotlessly clean. Energy saving and ultra-quiet, with innovative PerfectDry technology that dries your dishes thoroughly - even on plastics! Discover the products from the world's number 1 dishwasher brand*.

Energy-efficient and built to last, our washing machines, dryers and all-in-one washer dryers perfectly clean your clothes, load after load.

+ BOSCH KBN96VFE0 SERIES 4 XXL BUILT -IN FRIDGE-FREEZER

BOSCH
Invented for life

040 - KITCHEN FURNITURE & SIGNATURE ITEMS

As a founding Director of Callerton in conjunction with my friend and business partner Gordon-Stanger-Leathes, some 40+ years ago - I thought it apt this final section of the book should incorporate input from him, alongside our CEO Dawn Short. It's been quite a journey and hopefully 'Insights' provides you with an appreciation of the World of the design-led kitchen specialist?

Gordon's opening comment relates to two enduring themes and principles apropos Callerton's approach, ethos, culture and outlook to business: -

"Our long-time strap line and belief in relation to 'Turning Dreams to Reality' has never wavered and as true today as it was 40 or so years ago. Also in relation to a further much used Callerton phrase as to our desire to be - 'The Furniture Manufacturer of Choice for the Design-led Kitchen Specialist".

We as a company have stood behind our principles (as per Gordon's statement) for over 40 years – and our longevity is testament to our commitment to the importance of the above. Dawn wished to incorporate Callerton's mission statement: - To ensure we continually strive in relation to being a 'Professional, Progressive, Sustainable and Resilient' entity.

I believe Gordon and Dawn's comments provide an insight as to the guiding principles of our business.

A further point from Dawn related to our commitment to education and expansion of knowledge in relation to our trade – as well as the significance of 'Right First Time'. As seen throughout 'Insights' – the skill, ability and complexity to create a design inspired dream kitchen is vast. Hence Callerton developing their own in-depth training programme to pursue this salient aspect of our craft.

The importance of all our staff, the Callerton Team (both past and present) enabling us to create an enterprise from scratch (to what it is today) is ably supported and demonstrated by all the many projects included in the book – this a further point Gordon wished to make.

Dawn shone a light on the significance of partnerships and relationships in Callerton's evolution. As she pointed out engagement with our National Network of Design-led Kitchen Specialist Retailers, our many Suppliers and Service Providers – all critical aspects of our business.

We decided to finish with an area close to Gordon and my own heart – ongoing development of product. The design-led kitchen industry is inextricably linked to fashion, which never stands still and constantly evolves - an aspect of our craft which makes it so engrossing.

We don't believe we need to show you any more projects as all the many 'Insights' kitchen case-studies incorporate Callerton furniture – so we thought imagery spotlighting various signature pieces and features would be an appropriate way to conclude.

Turning Dreams to Reality' has never wavered & is as true today as it was 40 or so years ago

Callerton

Turning Dreams to Reality

20 LESSONS LEARNT OVER 50 YEARS OF WORKING LIFE

I decided to finish my book by utilising an extract from a speech I gave when standing down as Callerton's Chairman and joined the ranks of the semi-retired (I should explain my long suffering Wife doesn't recognise or allow me to use the word retired). The intention to pass on a small 'Insight' to anyone following in my footsteps, as to how I've approached the world of work. If you extract half as much fun out of out of your career as I have – you will have an absolute ball.

ADDENDUM

There's no I or Me in Team.
The power of a Positive & Capable Team - immense

Negativity the
preserve of
the masses –
Originality &
Positivity
a rarer
commodity

1 - Negativity the preserve of the masses – Originality & Positivity a rarer commodity.

2 - Everyone can tell you what you can't do – be willing to stand by your Judgement & Dream.

3 - Health & Happiness inevitably out-do Wealth & Status - in my experience.

4 - Develop a Work/Life Balance incorporating Family & Friends - something I subscribe to.

5 - Learn to Listen, leave a meeting with a view opposite to that which you entered - uplifting.

6 - Simple Good Manners & an ability to say Sorry when duly required – a powerful tool.

7 - A Well Done or Thank You in appreciation of a job well done – of immeasurable value.

8 - There's no I or Me in Team. The power of a Positive & Capable Team - immense.

9 - Without a focused Aim & Goal, plus a subsequent Strategy & Action Plan – likelihood of failure increases.

10 - Drive & Passion, & an ability to impart these - critical ingredients for a successful business.

11 - Engagement with Education & Learning to eradicate issues in advance – pays major dividends.

12 - Communication Skills & the ability to develop Meaningful Relationships – vital in the World of Work.

13 - Building Trust & Partnerships – important ingredients throughout my career.

14 - Input & Effort without achieving a Result – tends to be a waste of resource.

15 - Identify your Strengths & Weaknesses – & work with others to mitigate your frailties.

16 - From a management perspective – Respect & Creditability more important than being liked.

17 - Humour & Humility – play their role in resolving issues & engendering a sense of fun.

18 - Ensure your Word is Meaningful, if you say you're going to do something - make sure it happens.

19 - An imbedded positive can-do Ethos & Culture throughout an organisation – works wonders.

20 - The Development of Friendships with Industry Colleagues – has played an important role in my career.

Building Trust & Partnerships –
important ingredients throughout my career

Health &
Happiness
inevitably out do
Wealth & Status -
in my experience

James R.A. Herriot

Darren Chung
has been my
go-to photographer
and friend for 20+
years... Darren has
played a vital role
in the history &
development
of Callerton

Great imagery is a major element and requirement to engage with all the wide-ranging options and possibilities when creating a Dream Kitchen. Words can only help to set the scene, 3D CAD imagery plays its vital part – but without great photography it is difficult to comprehend the magic of what the finished article can truly engender. Great photography is an art-form and a vital aspect in demonstrating our craft: - Hence I wish to recognise and thank all those amazing photographers who have contributed to 'Insights to Kitchen Design' – without you the book would not exist.

Darren Chung has been my go to photographer and friend for 20+ years. All the 'Insights' photography relating to the kitchen case-studies I had involvement, as well as a great many more, were at the talented hands of Darren. I must take this opportunity to thank him for all his help and assistance over the years - Darren has played a vital role in the history and development of Callerton.

The photography of a number of the case-studies involving the 10 Design-led Kitchen Specialists from Callerton's National Network (featured within 'Insights') was carried out by photographers they had engaged. I would like to take this opportunity to acknowledge their input and to thank them.

The following is a list of the kitchen case-studies and the relevant photographer: -

Project 017 - Minimalist Marvel – Charlotte Wright Photography

Project 018 - Salutary Style – Kate Buckingham Photography

Project 019 - Party Central – Ralph Media Group Ltd

Project 020 - Perfect Situation – Harvey Bell Photography

Project 025 - Graceful Opulence – Paul Mavor Photography

PHOTO-GRAPHY

INSIGHTS

TO KITCHEN DESIGN

40+ Years in the World of a
Design-led Kitchen Specialist

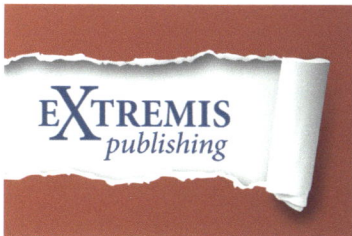

EXTREMIS
publishing

James R.A. Herriot

FOR THOSE WISHING TO SEE ANOTHER SIDE TO THE AUTHOR –

THE SABBATICAL:
A Year of Travel During the Pandemic

If you were able to travel anywhere in the world, where would you go? During the 2nd Covid-19 pandemic lockdown, James Herriot decided to collate various of the journeys he and his wife (Debbie) have made during their life together as a journal for the grandchildren. Reminiscing about their favourite places, James also includes suggestions for good books, his favourite music, as well as fine wines consumed with family and friends in the various locations.

Travel with him from his beautiful home town of Berwick-upon-Tweed to Australia, New Zealand, America, Italy, France, Croatia, Turkey, and others, plus some closer to home – all 52 having their own story to tell. Sometimes humorous, sometimes sad, his observations are always thought provoking. The Sabbatical will help you to reminisce about places you have visited – or possibly encourage you to visit them for yourself.

www.thesabbatical.co.uk

James & Debbie Herriot

For details of new and forthcoming books from Extremis Publishing, including our monthly podcast, please visit our official website at:

www.extremispublishing.com

or follow us on social media at

www.facebook.com/extremispublishing

www.linkedin.com/company/extremis-publishing-ltd-/

EXTREMIS
publishing

www.ingramcontent.com/pod-product-compliance
Lightning Source LLC
Chambersburg PA
CBHW041226020426

42333CB00005B/62